THE BRIDGE AT LO WU

DESMOND FORRISTAL

The Bridge at Lo Wu

A Life of Sister Eamonn O'Sullivan

VERITAS

First published 1987 by
Veritas Publications
7-8 Lower Abbey Street
Dublin 1

Copyright © Desmond Forristal 1987

ISBN 0 86217 268 3

Cover design: Don Farrell
Typesetting: Printset & Design Ltd., Dublin
Printed in the Republic of Ireland by
Mount Salus Press Limited

Contents

FOREWORD

Shortly after the outbreak of the Chinese Cultural Revolution, I found myself in the railway station at Lo Wu on the border between Hong Kong and China. I was there as part of a film team making a series of documentaries about the Church in the Far East. We had hoped to visit China but the Cultural Revolution had plunged the country into turmoil and foreigners were unwelcome, especially foreigners with film cameras. The nearest we could get was Lo Wu.

Our guide at Lo Wu was a friendly Irishman, Superintendent Matt O'Sullivan of the Hong Kong Police. He had witnessed many memorable moments at Lo Wu, some joyful, some tragic, as missionaries expelled from China walked the 200 yards across the railway bridge to freedom. Some of them were so weak and emaciated after years in prison that even that short walk was too much for them.

His most recent and vivid memory was of the expulsion of eight Franciscan nuns on 31 August 1966. Their convent in Peking had been sacked and they themselves subjected to a week of terror and abuse. He decribed how one of them collapsed on leaving the train and the others had to push her across the bridge on a baggage trolley. She died less than twenty-four hours afterwards. Like him, she came from Cork. Like him, her name was O'Sullivan.

For twenty years it was not possible to tell the full story of Sister Eamonn O'Sullivan and her companions. The Chinese sisters in the convent had been sentenced to twenty years in prison and it was feared that further publicity might only add to their sufferings. That situation has now changed. The twenty years have passed, the three surviving sisters are more or less at liberty, and the present Chinese government is trying cautiously to distance itself from the cruelty and injustice of the Mao Tse-tung regime.

In writing this life of Sister Eamonn, it is not my intention to portray her as an exceptional or outstanding figure. She was a small, fat nun who liked to laugh a lot. It is her very ordinariness that makes her important. Her life is typical of an era that is far different from ours even though it is so close to us in time. This portrait of her is a portrait of a whole generation of Irish men and women who grew up in an atmosphere of prayer and faith and who shaped their lives by that faith to the end of their days.

There are some people I must thank for help in the writing of this book. I am indebted to the Superior and community of Loughglynn Convent, especially Sister Mary Anne McArdle, and to the librarians of the Dublin Diocesan Library, Royal Dublin Society Library and Bray Public Library. Above all, I am indebted to Sister Eamonn's sister, Nance O'Sullivan, who is now Sister Eucharia of the Ursuline Convent in Brecon, Wales.

During the past twenty years, Sister Eucharia has gathered together her sister's letters, along with reminiscences from her family and friends, newspaper cuttings, magazine articles, photographs and other relevant material. In addition, she has written down in rich detail her own memories of her sister and especially of the happy childhood they shared together in Cork. All this material she has placed unconditionally at my disposal. I hope this book will prove worthy of her trust.

1
A CORK CHILDHOOD

Molly O'Sullivan was born at 8 Balmoral Terrace, Cork, on 26 March 1907, the eldest of a family of ten. Her parents, Ned O'Sullivan and Nora Kiely, had been married the previous June in the Cathedral in Cork.

Ned O'Sullivan, her father, was well-used to large families. He himself came from a family of eighteen children. Among them, the closest one to him was his sister Annie and the first great sorrow he experienced as a young man was when he learned that she was suffering from tuberculosis and was not expected to live. Her great wish before she died was to see her beloved brother happily married and she told him she knew someone who would gladly marry him and would make him a good wife. That someone was her friend Nora Kiely.

From that day on, Ned had his eye on Nora. Although he had never spoken to her, he liked what he saw. One day in the summer of 1904 he and his cousin, Tom Power, were walking down a street in Cork when they saw Nora approaching, 'Do you see this girl coming towards us?' he said quietly to Tom. 'I don't know her yet, but she's the girl I'm going to marry.'

Although officially Nora knew nothing about this secret admirer, it is hardly likely that she was completely unaware of his interest in her. However, it was up to him to make the first move and she had to wait as patiently as she could for him to take the plunge. It wasn't until the autumn of 1905 that their first meeting took place. It proved to be decisive.

On that never-to-be-forgotten evening, Ned was having a quiet smoke near the gate of his home, Ballyvolane House, when he saw a girl coming along the road on a bicycle from the direction of Carrignavar. As she drew near, he saw that it was Nora. Mustering up his courage, he stepped out into the road and intercepted her. She stopped, got off her bicycle and spoke for the first time to her future husband.

It was a brief conversation but before it ended they agreed to meet later that evening and go for a walk together. The walk went on for a long time and neither of them was in any hurry to end it. When they finally arrived back at Nora's home, Ned had made up his mind. 'I'm not walking you out for fun, Nora', he said, 'I intend to marry you — if you'll have me.' Nora had made up her mind too and the matter was settled there and then. It only remained to decide on the time and place of the wedding.

They were married on 20 June 1906, in St Mary's Cathedral. It was a quiet wedding, since Ned was still in mourning for his sister Annie, who had died just three months earlier. Before her death, she had the happiness of knowing that her match-making efforts had been successful. Ned was now thirty years of age and his bride was six years younger.

After a short honeymoon in England, the couple returned to Cork to their new home at St Luke's, 8 Balmoral Terrace. Ned had a good job as a pig-buyer for the firm of Marsh & Baxter, Birmingham, and he was also a part-time buyer for the Irish firms of Denny's and Lunham's. He worked hard and spent much of his time travelling around the south of Ireland from one fair to another, which meant that he was often away from home for four or five nights at a time. Despite these absences, or perhaps all the more because of them, Ned was devoted to his wife and children and their family life was to prove a very happy one.

Within a few weeks of their return, Nora discovered that she was pregnant and started saying the Thirty Days' Prayer, a traditional devotion for mothers-to-be. That prayer was to be her stand-by during each of her ten pregnancies. Like her husband, Nora was a devoutly religious Catholic. At one time she had hoped to enter the Little Sisters of the Poor but was prevented by the duty of nursing first a dying grandmother and then a dying uncle. Finally, when Ned arrived on the scene, she decided that God was calling her not to be a nun but a good Catholic wife and mother and such she remained until the end of her long life.

Their first child was born in Balmoral Terrace on 26 March

1907. The following day the baby girl was baptised in the church at Mayfield, chapel-of-ease to the parish of of St Patrick's. She was christened Mary but her father soon decided to call her Molly and the name stuck.

Within a year, Nora was pregnant again. Her second child, a boy, was born towards the end of 1908 and given the name Declan. Around this time, Nora's unmarried uncle Pat, known to the family as Nunk, also came to live with them. The house at Balmoral Terrace was now becoming overcrowded and they began to look around for something roomier. They found a suitable house in Thomas Davis Street in the Blackpool area of Cork. Not only was the house larger, but it had the additional advantage of a large yard with extensive outhouses where Ned could keep pigs awaiting shipment to England.

The move did not prove to be a happy one. Misfortune seemed to hang over the new house. Nora's third child, Kitty, weighed only three and a half pounds when she was born in May 1910, and it was feared for a time that she would not live. Then Uncle Pat contracted typhoid fever and lay for a long time at death's door before Nora's devoted nursing brought him back to health. Hardly was this second crisis past when Declan developed diphtheria. Neither prayers nor nursing could save his life and Ned and Nora had the sorrow of watching their little son die.

It is not surprising that Nora took a violent dislike to the house in Thomas Davis Street. She and Ned went house-hunting again and this time they were luckier in their choice. They bought a good-sized house and yard in Dublin Street where they were to spend eleven happy years and where their next six children were to be born; three more daughters, Nance, Norrie and Enda, then two longed-for sons, Barry and Eamonn and, finally, one more daughter, Pam.

* * *

The home in which Molly O'Sullivan grew up was a typical middle-class home of that place and period. Cork in the early years of the twentieth century was a small but prosperous city, even if its prosperity was unevenly divided. The O'Sullivans were not rich but they were certainly comfortable. The children were always well-fed, well-clothed and well-housed. There was usually a servant girl to help with the housework and a couple of men employed in the piggery. Every year the family spent the summer holidays at one of the nearby seaside resorts.

The city prided itself on its cultural life. In addition to many good schools, it had the newly established University College, a constituent college of the National University of Ireland. It also had the Cork Opera House which played host to all the leading theatrical companies of the day and provided a wide choice of opera and drama for its patrons. The people of Cork were more familiar with the works of Verdi and Shakespeare in those days than they are now.

It was an overwhelmingly Catholic city. Unlike the more cosmopolitan Dublin, it had few Protestants and fewer Jews. The year revolved around the great fasts and feasts of the Church: Advent, Christmas, Epiphany, Lent, Holy Week, Easter, Pentecost. It culminated in the Feast of Corpus Christi with its great outdoor procession of the Blessed Sacrament, an act of corporate faith and devotion which seemed to involve the entire city and everyone in it.

These influences were reflected in the O'Sullivan household. From her earliest days, Molly lived in an atmosphere of prayer and piety. The family rosary was said every night and the children took their part in it as soon as they were old enough to say the 'Hail Mary' and hold the beads in their hands. The traditional coloured pictures of the Sacred Heart and the Blessed Virgin hung on their bedroom walls. During the Christmas season there was a crib on top of the chest of drawers with the three kings making their dramatic appearance on 6 January. In May the same chest of drawers was topped by a spotless linen cloth in order to become the May altar. On it was placed the statue of the Blessed Virgin, with two candles and vases of fresh flowers from Kate McCarthy's florist shop. All year round, a red lamp glowed in front of the Sacred Heart picture, the last thing the children saw before they fell asleep.

Nora was a daily Mass-goer. Every morning, winter or summer, she was at the six o'clock Mass in the Assumption Convent. The children were welcome to accompany her but the choice was up to them. They were given no choice about the weekly Confession and every Saturday morning at ten o'clock they were marched off to Blackpool chapel for the children's Confessions.

Sunday Mass and Holy Communion was the most important

event of the week. Ned, whose parents came from Tralee, observed two old Kerry customs relating to the receiving of Communion. The night beforehand, all those who were to receive washed their feet or had their feet washed for them even if they had already bathed, in memory of Christ washing the apostles' feet at the Last Supper. On Sunday morning when they returned home after Mass, each of the family drank a glass of pure water before sitting down to breakfast. These simple but deeply-felt customs impressed on the children's minds a reverence for the Blessed Eucharist that was to last all their lives.

Molly made her own first Holy Communion at the age of six. Two years earlier she had started her education at the local national school. Within a year her teacher, Mrs O'Mahony, was preparing her for her first Confession and Communion. Pope Pius X had recently lowered the age for receiving the sacraments and a child was permitted to make its first Communion as soon as it was mature enough to recognise the difference between the Eucharist and ordinary bread.

The local dress-maker, Mrs McMahon, was called in to provide Molly's first Communion outfit. She was a tall, thin lady who made all the children's coats and dresses and was a familiar figure in the house. She put Molly up on the table for her first fitting, while the younger sisters stood around and watched the spectacle.

'So you're all going to be nuns?' said Mrs McMahon by way of agreeable conversation. 'And who's going to be the reverend mother?' she added, twirling Molly around and sticking in another couple of pins. The little girl had no ambitions of this sort and sang out in the words of the old song:

> No, I won't be a nun,
> No, I won't be a nun,
> I'll get married in the morning
> And I won't be a nun.

When the morning came she did almost look as if she were going to get married as she left the house in her white veil and white gloves and long white dress. The traditional 'covered car', a horse-drawn cab, drove her to the Cathedral where the ceremony was to take place. She and her school-mates took their places in the front seats of the church and joined in the familiar prayers and hymns before going up to the altar rails to receive the Eucharist.

Jesus, thou art coming,
Holy as thou art,
Thou the God who made me
To my little heart.

She returned to her place with hands joined and head bowed to make her thanksgiving. In later years her sister and brothers were to notice and marvel at her reverence both before and after receiving the Eucharist. More than fifty years would separate her first Communion from her last, but during all that time the Blessed Sacrament never ceased to be the centre and mainstay of her spiritual life. Her first Communion took place with every pomp and ceremony, in a church decked with flowers and candles and filled with family and friends; her last in grotesque and terrifying circumstances, amid the threats and blasphemies of a hostile mob. But to the eyes of faith, it was the same Lord who was present each time under the appearance of the small white host.

* * *

As the years passed, Molly grew into a cheerful and vivacious girl. Rather short and plump, she was of the type then known as 'petite'. Though she could not be described as beautiful, her face was attractive, especially when she smiled, which she did often. She herself regarded her rich chestnut-brown hair as her best feature.

Her temperament was open and sunny. She was not a worrier and when things went wrong her favourite saying was, 'It'll all be the same in a hundred years' time', which could prove somewhat irritating to those who were concerned about the more immediate future. She loved company and was the life and soul of every party. Her enjoyment was so spontaneous and uninhibited that it made others enjoy themselves too. In particular, all her friends recalled her keen sense of humour and her very characteristic laugh, which had a habit of breaking out on inappropriate occasions. It had an infectious quality which made others join in and often got her into trouble at school and later on in the convent.

She enjoyed sport and was specially fond of camogie, tennis and swimming, even if her short legs prevented her from excelling. She had plenty of intelligence and common sense but could hardly be described as an intellectual. There was only one area in which she was exceptionally gifted and that was music.

Molly started to sing almost as soon as she started to talk. Nora was quick to recognise her talent and she arranged for her to start taking piano lessons from a cousin, Noelle Duggan, when she was only four. Before she was six, she sat for her first music examination. The exam took place in the Imperial Hotel and the little girl was escorted there by her proud mother. She passed the exam with honours and in due course an elaborate certificate from the Royal Irish Academy of Music arrived to attest the fact. The following year she also began to take violin lessons although the piano always remained her first love.

Practising the piano in a house full of children had its difficulties. While Molly toiled through her scales and arpeggios in the sitting room, her younger sisters were romping in the dining-room just across the hall. After a few minutes Molly, who hated missing any kind of jollity, would clamber down from the piano stool and come across to join in the fun. Eventually she agreed to let herself be locked in for a half an hour at a time so that she could practise her scales and pieces for her next lesson.

At the age of ten, she left the National School and went to St Aloysius's School, run by the Sisters of Mercy, which she was to attend for the next eight years. Among the extras provided by St Aloysius's was a Saturday dancing class and the combination of music and movement was a delightful new experience for Molly. The dancing mistress, Mrs Lyons, was regarded by the O'Sullivan girls as the last word in sophistication. Molly's sister, Nance, remembers her vividly.

> She was a flamboyant personality. In appearance she was very much like what Molly was to become when grown up: petite, plump, with beautiful hands and feet. She always made an 'entrance' to the dancing class. Coming late, broad mink stole (with nest of violets) flying, she began to pull off her white gloves at the door, using her jewelled hands to great effect.

The following year Molly was confirmed at the Lough parish church. For the whole of that school year, religion was the most important subject. The candidates for Confirmation had to master a very full course in doctrine and scripture. The entire text of the Catechism had to be known by heart. In addition, the pupils had to be familiar with two other books, *Catechism Notes*, and *Schuster's Bible History*. In later years, she was to refer with gratitude to the firm grounding in the fundamentals of her faith which that year's study had given her.

Four months before her death, she wrote letters from Peking to two young nephews preparing for Confirmation. To one of them she said:

> Do you really know and realise what Confirmation is? It is to become a strong and perfect Christian. You must be ready to suffer to save your soul and the souls of others. This day is not just a day on which you receive all kinds of new clothes and presents but a day on which you receive extra special graces from God. Very often we forget the great love he has for us. We are his children whether we are old or young and every event joyful or sorrowful comes from his loving hand with the necessary grace to do his Will.
>
> Every human being is tried in a furnace of suffering to see if he is fit for the kingdom of heaven. If he is not, he is rejected like Saul. Do you know who Saul is? If you don't, ask your teacher in school. Remember our eternity depends on ourselves; on myself, not on my father or mother or brother but on myself. Today you have received a very great grace to help you for your eternity. Go to Confession and Holy Communion often and you will secure your hereafter. All I've said in this letter is very serious: but life is very serious and our eternity more so.
>
> Goodbye now, Patrick, and be a very good boy, for heaven's at the end of the road.

*   *   *

'We had a very happy childhood', said one of Molly's sisters. That note of happiness comes out very strongly in the reminiscences of all those who knew the O'Sullivan household, whether they were members of the family or not.

It began with the parents. Ned and Nora were both devoted to their children in their different ways. Of the two, Nora was the more dominant personality. She was the decision-maker in everything that affected the family. The house was her domain and she ruled it with kindness but also with firmness. She did

16

not hesitate to punish when punishment was due. She knew what she wanted for herself, for her husband and for her children, and she let no obstacles stand in her way.

Ned was a softer and gentler personality. When he returned to the house, often after three or four days on the road, there were no problems of discipline to be sorted out and to cast a cloud over his homecoming. Nora had dealt with these and all other outstanding business in his absence. As soon as he was heard at the hall door, a torrent of small girls rushed out to meet him. One took his hat, another his coat, a third his walking-stick. Molly, as the eldest, had the privilege of taking his Gladstone bag and stowing it safely away. One of her sisters later paid a touching tribute to his personality.

> It was easy in this family where there was so much love to be ever-conscious of the fatherhood of God. Molly's great love for her father was not unique in the family. All his children idolised him. Every enjoyment was keener, every song was sweeter, every dawn was brighter, when Dad was there. The '*Kepler's Malt and Cod Liver Oil*' was special when he administered it. He had a tender way with small children and could pick up a child who had fallen asleep at supper — not an unusual occurrence — and could undress and put her to bed without waking her.
>
> Ned had most beautiful hands, O'Sullivan hands, long but not narrow, beautifully formed and shaped. They were peculiarly innocent hands, expressive of his goodness, his character and his judgement, which were trusted without question by all his children. He never had to lay down the law. In the eyes of his family he was always right.

The big house, with its even bigger yard and outhouses, was a paradise for small children. The three-storey house had a sitting-room, dining-room and kitchen on the ground floor, with a glass conservatory at the back. There were bedrooms and a bathroom on the floor above, and on the top floor another two large bedrooms, lit by dormer windows. On Saturday afternoons, when Nora was paying her weekly visit to the matinee at the Opera House, a favourite adventure of the children was to climb out of the bathroom window and see how far they could walk along the roofs of the outhouses. The older girls usually got back safely into the house but the yardman often had to bring out his ladder to rescue the younger ones. No word of these exploits ever reached Nora's ears.

The outhouses included several piggeries, a pig-infirmary, three straw-lofts and a boiler-house. The children avoided the infirmary, as the sight of sick animals upset them, but they loved playing hide-and-seek in the straw-lofts. Best of all was the boiler-house, especially on Sunday mornings when the vats had been emptied and cleaned.

Nance remembers being chosen as victim in the game of 'Cannibal Chief' when she was still little more than a toddler. The cannibals put her into one of the vats and then the cannibal chief asked her for her name.

'What do you want to know my name for?' she asked.
'To put it on the menu!' was the reply.

At this she burst into tears and had to be taken out and brought to her mother, who ruled that this particular game was not to be played any more.

As the girls grew older, they were sometimes allowed to accompany Nora to the Opera House matinee. They learned to appreciate all kinds of music and theatre; grand opera, light opera, musical comedies, classical concerts, jazz concerts, dramas, comedies and farces. For Molly, the grand opera seasons were the greatest attractions. Several London-based opera companies visited Cork regularly: the Carl Rosa Company, the Moody Manners Company and the Joseph O'Meara Company. In addition to the standard nineteenth-century operas, they were introducing new works by the latest favourite, Puccini.

Molly's own musicianship was developing steadily. At the age of fourteen, she started taking piano lessons from a leading Cork teacher, Professor George Brady. To celebrate the occasion, her mother bought a walnut-cased baby grand and installed it in the sitting-room. Her singing voice was also maturing under the guidance of Nora's sister, Annie O'Connor. Auntie Annie had a collection of records by leading opera singers of the day and she would get Molly to listen to their rendering of an aria and then encourage her to try and sing it herself. 'Moll, that was great,' she would say approvingly at the end of the session. 'And you are pitch-perfect, which Galli-Curci is not!'

As the eldest in the family, Molly was expected to help in looking after her younger sisters and brothers. She washed them, put them to bed, said their prayers with them, told them a bed-time story or sang them to sleep. Whenever Nora was looking for a little peace in the house, Molly was told to take the others for a walk. They enjoyed these outings. Even on wet winter days, they would head off happily along the Mallow road or Dublin Hill or the road to Ballyvolane, kitted out in hooded mackintosh coats and rubber boots. When they returned home, a roaring fire was waiting to greet them together with a change of clothes and a bowl of steaming hot soup.

Apart from the usual childish ailments, the family enjoyed good health in Dublin Street. The decision to remove all the children's tonsils in 1919, when Molly was twelve, seems to have been prompted more by current medical fashion than by any real physical need. A well-known Cork physician, Dr. P. T. O'Connor, was in charge of the operation, which took place in the house. The children watched with fascinated apprehension as their executioners arrived. First the gas-cylinder was carried upstairs to one of the bedrooms. Then the doctor followed with a terrifying array of instruments and sterilisers. Finally, a portable operating table was brought in, unfolded and set up. The anaesthetic was briskly administered, the offending organs were whipped out, and the doctor with his assistants and paraphernalia had vanished before the victims recovered consciousness. The operation proved that the O'Sullivan parents were prepared to spare no expense on behalf of their children. It seems to have had no other beneficial effects whatever.

2

PEACE AND WAR

Every year the family went for a long holiday to the seaside. For the first few years of Molly's life, they rented a house on or near the promenade in Youghal in east County Cork. To help with her growing brood, Nora usually brought along her friend Nannie McMahon, affectionately known to the children as Nannie Mac.

In 1916 two adjoining cottages came on the market in Ferry Point, County Waterford, just across the estuary from Youghal, and were snapped up by Nora. Under her supervision, a local handyman transformed them into a pleasant little holiday home. The two cottages were made into one, the windows were enlarged, and a glass door was installed at the back leading to a small garden which overlooked the sea. The new house was named St Enda's in tribute to the memory of the recently executed Patrick Pearse, who had founded a school of that name. Nance writes about those happy times:

> Holidays at Ferry Point were halcyon days, carefree, innocent, full of song and laughter. The family all but lived on the strand at Monatrae. Ned, an expert swimmer, taught the children to swim almost as soon as they could walk. Molly and the elder girls frequently went with Ned to Carty's Cove, where the rocks were steep, ideal for diving. Surfacing from seven or eight feet of water with eyes wide open as they had been taught, they scrambled up the rocks to dive again and again in this safe but very deep water.
>
> Behind St Enda's, the sea rose so high at full tide that daily diving practice could be obtained off the high

surrounding wall. Any small child taking the high dive who cut the water sweetly without splashing won not only praise but an occasional penny.

Picnic days were a child's dream, and almost every fine day except Sunday and Monday were potential picnic days. Nora, with her weather eye open, had only to say, 'Would anyone like to go to Whiting Bay?' and all were galvanised into activity. Whether it was Caliso Bay, Whiting Bay or Goat's Island didn't matter. This was a picnic!

There was no family car in those days and someone ran to get Johnny Roche's donkey. The donkey car was loaded with provisions, small children and gramophone, and those who had bicycles stacked the carriers with swimming gear. When the grown-ups, who had to use Shank's Mare, were ready, the whole retinue moved off like a small regiment. The long summer's day until dusk was spent on the strand, children in and out of the water like little otters, eating sandy sandwiches, fetching kettles of water, and on windy days forming a human screen to coax the Primus to behave.

By the time she reached her teens, Molly, like her father, had become a strong and expert swimmer. A curious incident around this time gave her the idea of trying to swim across the estuary from Youghal to Ferry Point. One day a baker, dressed in his white suit and obviously drunk, rushed down the boatslip in Youghal, shouting that he was going to swim across the estuary. Before anyone could stop him, he had plunged into the sea. It was a long and dangerous swim, especially in the central channel, where the river met the rising tide and formed treacherous currents and eddies. Some of the boatmen on the quay immediately put out after him but, when they at last caught up with him, he refused all offers of rescue. As he was very large and drunk and determined and could easily cause the boat to capsize, they could do nothing except tail along behind him. Eventually his feet touched bottom and he walked up the strand on the other side, by now sober enough to be appalled at what he had just done. There was no difficulty in persuading him to return to Youghal by boat.

Molly decided that what could be done by a drunken baker should be well within the capability of a sober O'Sullivan. She enlisted a rather reluctant Nance and the two of them spent long

21

hours every day training for the big event. They reached the stage where they could swim a mile along the shore from St Enda's and another mile back. At this point, however, Ned found out about the plan and put his foot down very firmly. The swim had to be abandoned, much to the disappointment of Molly if not of Nance.

The summer days at Ferry Point developed a routine of their own. Water had to be fetched from the well, milk from a nearby farm. Another farmer provided vegetables and a local fisherman pulled in to the Point each morning at dawn to sell his catch of the previous night.

Fetching the water was quite an adventure. The well was in a field which also contained Keane's bull, a large and reputedly savage animal. The bucket-carrier had to wait until the bull's back was turned, then make a quick dash to the well, fill the bucket, and dash back to the safety of the ditch before the bull could make a charge. The inexpert and the nervous often lost most of the water in the rush. The younger children found it an ordeal but Molly enjoyed the challenge and would saunter nonchalantly to the well and back again. On at least one occasion she barely reached the shelter of the ditch in time.

Going for the milk meant having a chat with J. P. Prendergast. J. P. was a bachelor and a reformed alcoholic. He was a deeply religious man who lived the life of a monk, never leaving the farm except to go across in the ferry for the early Mass in Youghal every Sunday morning. The children often found him in the kitchen, enveloped in a huge blue apron, flour up to his elbows as he made the daily bastible cake, or bending over a tub of washing, soaping and rinsing until the linen was snow-white. He seemed to be able to understand the mind of a child, and he would speak to them about God with an ease and simplicity that touched their hearts. Every evening he would climb the hill behind the farm, and walk to and fro for an hour or two, silhouetted against the sky. From below, a child's sharp eyes could catch an occasional gleam when the setting sun caught the metal of the rosary beads swinging from his hands. He had a deep influence on Molly, and she believed that his hidden life of prayer was doing more for God and for souls than the sermons of many a famous preacher.

The last excursion of the summer was to Power's orchard in Pilltown for the winter's supply of apples. The whole family walked across the back strand to the orchard and spent the day picking apples, stripping one tree at a time. When the apples were paid for and put into sacks, Mr Power loaded them on to his cart and brought them by road to St Enda's.

The next day, the covered lorry arrived for the return to Cork. The lorry took the apples and other food, along with clothes and bedding and any particularly valuable items of furniture, such as the upright piano. Normally the family travelled separately, but on one memorable occasion Nora allowed some of the middle group of children to travel in the lorry with the household goods. The thirty-mile journey should not have lasted more than an hour or so but this time it lasted three. The driver was thirsty and seemed unable to pass a public house without stopping. The children inside grew increasingly restless and, after a particularly long wait in the main street at Midleton, one of the girls opened the piano and started to play. The others sang along at the tops of their young voices and within a short time they had attracted a crowd of curious onlookers. 'What's it for?' said someone at the back of the crowd, trying to peer into the darkness of the lorry. 'I think it's part of the circus', said someone else, to the unbounded delight of the performers.

Molly, who was not on the lorry, was equally delighted by the incident and for a long time afterwards used to refer to the family as 'the circus'. In its own way, that nickname seemed to sum up what she and all the others felt for their family, that sprawling, maddening, lovable octopus that held them all as willing captives in its embrace.

*   *   *

The years of Molly's adolescence were the years of the struggle for Irish independence. The O'Sullivan home was an intensely nationalist one, though characteristically it was the mother rather than the father who set the tone. Many of Ned's relatives were prominent in the movement and he himself was whole-heartedly sympathetic, but he felt his first duty was to his family and he never took any active part in politics. Nora, on the other hand, was passionately patriotic, could quote freely from Grattan, Thomas Davis and Parnell, and revelled in the cut and thrust of a good political argument.

The Easter Rising of 1916 and the subsequent execution of

its leaders made a deep impression on the O'Sullivan family, as it did on the whole country. The suppression of the rising was followed by an uneasy period of peace while the Irish people tried to decide which road to take, the road of constitutional opposition or the road of armed resistance. During this period a constant visitor to the house in Dublin Street was Joe Barrett from Tralee. He was Ned's cousin and often travelled with him as he made the circuit of the southern fairs. Joe was completely convinced that force was the only way and he was waiting impatiently for the call to arms.

Joe had a pleasing tenor voice and after supper with the O'Sullivans he used to entertain them with patriotic songs. He taught Molly many songs which were not easily available at that time and she eagerly wrote down the words of such pieces as *Who fears to speak of Ninety-eight?*, *The Rose of Tralee*, *The Bold Fenian Men*, *O'Donnell Abu* and *The West's Awake* and added them to her repertoire. When it came to bed-time, Nora would say, 'Give us *A Soldier's Song* now, Joe', and he would duly sing it. It was always an emotional moment. The song, not yet hackneyed in the way every national anthem is hackneyed, had about it the aura of a secret watchword. As they joined in, the O'Sullivans felt they were taking part in a rite of allegiance to their country and an act of solidarity with the patriots of the past.

Early in 1919 Eamon de Valera escaped from Lincoln Jail and assumed the leadership of the armed struggle. Flying columns were formed throughout the country and attacks on police and military barracks became widespread. Joe Barrett immediately joined the Volunteers, two of his younger brothers joined Fianna Éireann and three of his sisters joined Cumann na mBan. Some of the Ferry Point friends, notably Tom and Paddy Veale, were also on active service with the IRA. The O'Sullivan children, too young to join anything, could only look on in admiration and envy.

It was not long before they too were drawn into the struggle. Relatives and friends in the movement gradually began to use the house in Dublin Street as a convenient shelter and it soon became one of the recognised hiding-places in the city. The 'boys' knew that Nora always had a welcome for them, and that she kept an empty room ready and waiting, with a quick get-away over the kitchen roof. Night after night, two or three or more would slip into the yard through the wicket gate and make their way around to the kitchen door. If the family were asleep, they would let themselves in and make a meal for themselves on the gas stove before creeping quietly up to bed. The children got used to seeing strange men around the house and came to know many of the leading members of the Cork battalions.

On several occasions the military came to the house during their searches of the city, but Nora usually managed to stop them entering. Her technique was always the same. As soon as she heard the lorry stop outside the house, she would grab the current baby from the cradle and open the door with it in her arms, the picture of defenceless innocence. This always had a disconcerting effect on the officer.

'I'm sorry to disturb you, Madam, but I have information that you are harbouring some men in your house.'

'There's nobody here but myself and the children,' she would reply sweetly and indeed truthfully, since by now the boys were dropping off the roof of the outhouse into the field behind. Then she would stand aside and add, 'But don't take my word for it. Come in and see for yourself.'

The military officers were gentlemen and no match for Nora in guile, and they usually withdrew with apologies for having troubled her. Only once did they actually enter the house and search it and they found nobody and nothing. Nora had delayed them long enough at the door to make sure of that.

On one occasion she had the much less pleasant experience of being raided by the Black-and-Tans. Their approach was very different. As soon as the lorry stopped, they tumbled into the street, shouting and firing their guns into the air. Nora opened the door at once, this time without a baby in her arms, and explained helpfully that they had come to the wrong house.

'While you're searching here, they'll be getting away from So-and-so's,' she told them, naming an ardent loyalist down the street. The Tans listened carefully to the directions she gave them and then piled into the lorry and careered off again, with more shouting and cursing and shots in the air.

Molly, who was thirteen years old in 1920, was allowed to play her small part in the battle. She was often used as a courier to bring messages from one part of the city to another. A schoolgirl on a bicycle did not arouse much suspicion and she was rarely stopped or questioned. She had a near escape one day when she ran unexpectedly into a Black-and-Tan holdup near Bridge Street. She was holding a scrap of paper with an initialled message in her hand, but she managed to slip it into her mouth as she got off her bicycle. She had it chewed and swallowed before her turn came to be questioned and searched.

Even the youngest of the children were affected by the troubles. Some of the men they had come to know disappeared suddenly, either taken prisoner or killed in action. Thomas McCurtain, a member of Sinn Féin who was elected Lord Mayor of Cork, was a near neighbour. He endeared himself to the children through his habit of paying their fares whenever he met them on the tram. They were horrified when they heard one morning that he had been murdered in his bed by the Black-and-Tans.

Paddy Veale from Ferry Point was one of those arrested and imprisoned in Cork County Jail. Every week Molly was sent to the jail by her mother to bring him a parcel of food and cigarettes. After her death he recalled how she would stand at the prison gate and call out, 'Is Paddy Veale there?' She always waited for his answering shout before handing in her parcel.

There were many other memories of those days, some glorious, some tragic. There was the night in December 1920 when the Black-and-Tans burnt the whole centre of Cork City. The children were roused out of bed in case the fire moved in their direction and the house might have to be abandoned. They stood at the attic window and watched the sky turn red and then orange and then yellow as street after street went up in flames. There was the Saturday in May 1921 when they ran into a Black-and-Tan raid while they were coming back from Confession (no war was allowed to interfere with the children's religious practice). They stood outside the church and looked on as the Tans evicted whole families from their homes on the other side of the street and then set fire to the houses.

The saddest of all their memories concerned an incident that took place during their summer holidays at Ferry Point. St Enda's was often used as a refuge by friends and acquaintances who were on the run. One of these was a young man whom we shall call John Joe, though that was not his real name. He was fair-haired and handsome, a fine swimmer and dancer and a good companion. All the O'Sullivan girls worshipped him.

One day two members of No. 2 Cork Brigade arrived at the house and asked for John Joe.

'He's down the strand somewhere', said Nora. 'The children

will get him for you. I'll get you something to eat.' But they had no time to wait. They were on urgent business.

When John Joe appeared, they said, 'The Commandment wants to see you. A special job. We're holed up this side of Midleton. We've to be off at once.' John Joe turned towards his room to collect his gear. 'No need', they said. 'It'll be a quick job. You won't be staying long.'

Seven days later the two men turned up again, looking tired and sad. They walked down the road with Nora, where the children couldn't hear what they were talking about. Then they came back to the house and Nora packed some provisions which they took away with them along with all John Joe's belongings. As they closed the door behind them, she burst into a paroxysm of weeping which terrified the children.

When at last she gained control of herself, she said, 'Children, get your beads. We'll say the rosary for the repose of the soul of poor John Joe. He was killed in action a few days ago.'

It was only much later that she told some of them the full story. John Joe had not been killed by the British. He had been accused of passing information about his comrades to the authorities in return for money. He was tried before a brigade court, found guilty and shot.

John Joe's family were never allowed to know what had happened. His body was brought back to his parents for Christian burial and they were told that he had been killed in an ambush. To her dying day, Nora believed he was innocent.

In July 1921 a truce was signed with Britain, followed by a treaty in December. The treaty secured independence for twenty-six of the counties of Ireland but left the other six under British rule. Many of the freedom fighters refused to accept the treaty and a civil war broke out between the two factions. It was a sad time for Nora as she saw former friends and companions taking up arms against one another.

After the defeat of the anti-treaty forces, some of her old comrades found themselves on the run once again. She took no sides but her home was still open to any of her friends who were looking for a place of refuge. By now the family had moved to a new house in Little Island, which was close to Cobh and the trans-Atlantic liners. Here many of the hunted Irregulars spent their last sad days and nights in Ireland, before setting out for a new life in America.

Many years later, Nora was offered a medal and a pension by the Irish Government in recognition of her services to her country. In a characteristic gesture, she accepted the medal and refused the pension.

The experiences of those years made a profound impression on her children and especially on Molly, her eldest child. For one thing, Molly was left with a mistrust of Britain and all things British that she never fully succeeded in overcoming. More importantly, she was given in her mother an example of courage in adversity that must have been to the forefront of her mind during her own time of trial. No-one could live so close to so remarkable a woman and remain unchanged.

3

LITTLE ISLAND

The move to Little Island took place in 1922. For a long time
Ned had been thinking about buying a farm. He was convinced
that the only real security came from land. Recent events in
Ireland and abroad had strengthened this conviction. Investments
could lose their value, savings could be wiped out by inflation,
houses could be burnt down. The one permanent and
indestructible asset was land. He had a large and growing family
to care for and his health was beginning to decline. He began
to look around for a suitable property.

It was a good time for buying land. In the aftermath of Irish
independence, many land-owners who had British connections
or sympathies were selling their lands and leaving the country.
There were several attractive holdings for sale in the Cork area
and Ned inspected a number of them, usually accompanied by
one or other of his daughters. Finally he decided on a farm at
a place called Ballytrasna on Little Island.

Little Island, a short distance outside Cork city, hardly
deserves to be called an island at all. The narrow ribbon of water
that separates it from the mainland is crossed by several bridges
and the island is linked by rail as well as by road to the city.
The farm bought by Ned was close to the railway and included
a large, rambling farm-house, with sitting-room, dining-room,
kitchen, pantry, scullery, bathroom and six bedrooms. It was
provided with running water and sanitation, unusual at that time
in rural areas, but electricity had not yet arrived and oil-lamps
and candles were the only form of lighting. The house was about
a mile's walk from the railway station, which meant that Molly
and her sisters could continue to attend their schools and music
lessons in Cork.

It was somewhere around this time that Molly first began to think seriously about the religious life. She attended a retreat in her school given by a Dominican priest, Fr Finbarr Ryan, who later became Archbishop Ryan of Trinidad. He seems to have had a special gift for communicating with the adolescent mind and uncovering hidden springs of generosity and idealism. Molly felt herself drawn to give her life as completely as possible to the service of God and of souls. She was particularly attracted to the Little Sisters of the Assumption whose main work was nursing the sick poor in their homes.

Twenty years earlier, Molly's mother had felt a similar call but had been prevented from following it because of illness in her family. History was about to repeat itself. Nora, who was now pregnant for the tenth and last time, caught influenza which developed into pneumonia and then into empyema, a very dangerous infection of the lungs. She was taken to hospital and spent three months there, while doctors fought to save her life and the life of her baby.

The whole responsibility of running the household suddenly fell upon Molly, a schoolgirl just coming up to her sixteenth birthday. Even with the help of a woman who came in every day, there was an immense amount of work to be done in a house with two adults and eight children and no electricity or modern labour-saving devices. A cousin, Kate O'Connor, remembers calling to the house one evening and finding Molly standing at the kitchen table with a stack of newly washed clothes at one end and a pile of school-books at the other. She was trying to study her Shakespeare and do the ironing at the same time.

Nora was discharged from the hospital after three months and came back to the house but she was still very weak and did not return to full health for several years. Her main worry at this time was her baby. The doctor told her there was little chance of its being born alive, so she began praying to St Walburga, patroness of the sick, and asking that the baby would at least live long enough to receive the waters of Baptism. The baby, a beautiful little girl, was born alive and was immediately baptised with the name Walburga. Nora was warned that even if the child survived she would be an invalid, so she turned to St Walburga again. She began a novena asking that God would either take the baby to himself or give her the health to lead a normal life. On the last day of the novena, the baby died.

The baby was laid out in her white christening robe, surrounded by narcissi. The childen knelt around the cot, waiting for Ned to return from Cork with the miniature white coffin for her burial. When he lifted the little body and placed it in the coffin, they saw him break down in tears for the first time in their lives.

*   *   *

In the summer of 1925 Molly left school. Nora was still far from well after her illness of two years ago. There were now eleven people in the house, Nora and Ned, their eight surviving children and Uncle Pat. It was obvious to Molly where her duty lay and she put all thoughts of a religious vocation from her mind for the time being. It was God's will that she should stay in the house in Little Island and look after the family for as long as she was needed.

It was a disappointment but Molly was not the kind of person to brood about disappointments. She was to spend another ten years in Little Island, years filled with responsibility and hard work but also with plenty of happiness and enjoyment. Now at least she was free of the burden of schoolwork and could give to the running of the house her whole and undivided attention.

It took all her time to do it. There was the constant daily round of cooking, baking, washing, scrubbing, waxing, polishing, all done without the help of machines. There was the butter-making in the little dairy, with the heavy churn which had to be turned by hand. There was the annual orgy of jam-making, 300 lb in all. There was the dressing and washing and general care of the younger children, which their mother could no longer attend to. Instead, Nora looked after the making and mending for the family. She spent much of the time in her armchair, a black Gladstone bag full of socks by her side, and during the daylight hours no-one ever saw her without her knitting or darning needles in her hand. To the end of his life Ned never wore socks other than those knitted by his wife.

The children had a half-holiday from school every Saturday and Nora encouraged Molly to go into Cork for the afternoon and evening. She used to begin the afternoon with a game of tennis, and her regular partner was her sister Kitty, who had been her closest companion and friend from childhood days. She usually started by being late for the train and had to run most of the way from the house. Sometimes she would find the train already in the station with the automatic gate locked and would have to vault illegally over the gate and dive into the train as it pulled away from the platform.

After the game of tennis, they would have tea in Thomson's or the Pavilion and then she would make her way to one of the city's many churches for her weekly Confession. The evening was usually spent at the Opera House, especially if there was a season of grand opera on at the time or a cross-Channel company with the latest musical, such as *Rose Marie*, *The Student Prince* or *Lilac Time*. Then back home again by the last train, with a twenty-minute walk in the dark from the station to the house at Ballytrasna.

A strange incident happened one night on the walk home from the station. It was May Eve 1927 and Molly was coming back from the opera, having caught the 11.20 from Cork. On this occasion her companion was Nance, who describes what happened next:

> Coming towards Heartbreak Hill, we saw three small lights suddenly flare out at road level. The lights, three candles stuck in bottles, were placed in the form of a triangle right in the middle of the road. A man stood over each candle, and all three were chanting some incantation or spell in a weird, completely concentrated attitude which conveyed something palpably evil and sinister. It was exactly midnight and the approach of footsteps had not been allowed to divert whatever was afoot.

The girls did not interfere but hurried home as quickly as possible. They knew that the eve of May day was a traditional time for witchcraft and black magic. It seemed as if a curse was being called down on somebody and they hoped it was not on them. Coincidence or not, the next twelve months were to be the unluckiest in the history of the O'Sullivan farm. Cows died, pigs died, cattle died. The climax came one Sunday morning when the family were coming back from early Mass and saw the field behind the house scattered all over with white Wyandotte poultry. It was the whole year's rearing, all dead.

Summer holidays were spent as usual in Ferry Point. The friendship with the Veales had strengthened and the Veale farmhouse at Moord, about a mile from St Enda's, became almost a second home for the O'Sullivans. The house was always full of young people and Molly and her sisters enjoyed the company. They also helped in the work around the farm, especially the hay-making in late August. Molly and her sister Kitty became experts at handling the horses and the reaper-and-binder. When the day's work in the fields was over and the cows were milked, everyone gathered in the big farmhouse kitchen for a dance and a sing-song. Forty years later, Statia Veale looked back nostalgically on those summer days with Molly and her friends:

> We were really very happy with her and she was a real sport, out with the boys driving the horses on the machine, cutting corn and making hay, milking cows, planting potatoes, feeding baby calves, and a thousand other jobs around the yard. What fun twisting the separator, getting cream and milk, with tins of froth going in all directions! That was the fun, to try and throw it on the one that had the nicest frock and poor Moll would spare no-one.
>
> And then, when all was over, we retired to the old kitchen for a dance and sing-song with all the boys. We had Irish sets and step-dancing, shouting, jumping, and the house almost knocked down. We had our own dear friend Pat Hallahan playing puss music and Tim Foley playing the accordion and Molly's mother like a colleen oge dancing with all the boys and Thomas Veale would love to give her a good twist.
>
> We had Michael O'Donovan staying here in Moord on holidays, now Fr O'Donovan, a great friend of Moll's. One evening we were finishing work, Molly, her three sisters and a friend Chrissie Dorgan were hiding in the shed with tins of separated milk to throw on his beautiful suit. He had nowhere to go only jump a five-foot gate. Then the shouting and cheering hunting him, and after a long chase all would return to dance and sing some rebel songs, and Pat Hallahan was always here and used to love to hear her sing *The Boys of the First Brigade* and *The Boys of Kilmichael*, and Mrs Veale sitting in her old armchair, she loved to see her dance and sing, and when it came to 10.30 Moll was to the front, 'Time for home'. At times there was a

deaf ear turned on her and Mrs Veale would say, 'Moll, it's not too late yet. Another dance!' and Pat Hallahan would ask her to sing the good old rebel song,

At the cross of old Pilltown at midnight,
We met them with rifle and steel.

Nance remembers it a little differently. She thinks that they threw the froth on one another's hair, not on their clothes. 'Molly, knowing the labour of washing and ironing for six girls, would be the last person to wish to destroy or mess up someone's pretty dress. As for trying to destroy a young cleric's new suit — it doesn't bear thinking about!' The entertainment never went on too late as there was work to be done next day and the rosary had to be said before anyone went to bed. Of the young people who danced and sang in the kitchen at Moord, four were to become priests and six or seven nuns.

Back in Cork, Molly was beginning to develop a new interest. The city had its own opera company at this period, the Cork Operatic Society, familiarly known as 'the Operatic'. It was an amateur group which put on an average of two shows a year in the Opera House, drawn from the light opera and musical comedy repertoire. Molly's cousin, Nance Power, was a member of the Society and she suggested to Molly that she might like to join. The musical director was Professor Theo Gmur and he required candidates for admission to sing a popular drawing-room ballad of the time, *The Kerry Dances*. He considered it to be a good test piece because of the changes of mood and tempo which it involved. It was a song Molly had been singing for years. She sailed through the audition effortlessly and was admitted to 'the Operatic'.

Membership of the society was to mean a lot to Molly in the years that followed. Every spring and autumn they staged a new production and Molly took part in each one as a member of the chorus. She never accepted a solo part because of the extra commitment involved. It took her all her time to get to the chorus rehearsals, which started at 7.30 p.m. and finished just in time for her to catch the 10.30 train back to Little Island.

There was a spirit of friendship and camaraderie in the society that Molly found very pleasant. She in her turn was to prove a source of unfailing good humour to the others, especially on nights when things were going badly. Fan Cottrell, who was the

34

society's leading lady at the time, remembered running down the quay late for rehearsal and being cheered up when she heard Molly's unmistakable laugh coming from the open windows of the rehearsal room. 'I have never since heard such an infectious laugh', she wrote later. 'Molly had us all laughing when at times we used to be very close to tears. I'd say they could never have lasted so long in the convent in China without Sister Mary Eamonn, the one and only Molly O'Sullivan, the cure for all ills!'

With Theo Gmur as director, Molly took part in several of the currently popular musical comedies, such as *The Geisha, A Country Girl* and *San Toy*. In 1928 J. T. Horne took over the directorship and put on a number of the Gilbert and Sullivan operas, including *The Mikado, The Gondoliers, Patience, Ruddigore* and *The Pirates of Penzance*. Molly was impressed with the new director and took voice lessons with him which continued until she entered the convent.

She put these lessons to good use in the church at Glounthane, the parish church of Little Island, where she was invited to sing solos at Mass on the principal feast-days. Her voice had developed into a very pure and sweet mezzo-soprano and her rendering of such favourites as the Franck *Panis Angelicus* or the Bach-Gounod *Ave Maria* used to fill her family with pride. The proudest of all was Ned, her father, who felt that his daughter was making the best use of her gift when she sang in praise of the God who had given it to her.

4
VOCATION

After Molly left school, Ned and Nora sent the next girl, Kitty, as a boarder to the Ursuline Convent in Thurles, and the other sisters followed in their turn. When Kitty finished school in 1928 she came back to Little Island and took over the running of the farm, which Ned had been forced to neglect because of his other business commitments. She turned out a great success at the job and with the help of a couple of farm labourers she soon had the farm ticking over very efficiently. Molly continued to look after the house and family.

The third girl, Nance, finished school in 1930 and decided that she wished to enter the religious life. It was the custom at the time for nuns from various religious orders to visit the convent in Thurles and talk to the senior girls in the hope of attracting vocations. They met with varying success. 'One overseas superior', Nance recalls, 'stands out as a classic example of striking the wrong note where generous Irish youth is concerned. To the ambitious, she promised a university degree; to others, she held out a bait of fringe luxury, including strawberries and daily fruit in season; to all, a life of cultured good living.'

Nance was more impressed by some of the Irish missionary orders who offered a life spent in the service of the poor and outcast of the world. For a time she considered joining the Columban Sisters and going to China as a missionary but her final decision was in favour of the nuns she knew best. She came back to Little Island after finishing school and told her parents that she had decided to enter the Ursulines.

Ned and Nora were delighted with the news. It was a wonderful honour and privilege in their eyes that a daughter of theirs should consecrate her life to God in this way. Their only worry, which was shared by Molly, was that Nance might be a little too young and unfamiliar with the world to make such a decision. Nora and Molly set off on a shopping expedition to Cork and returned with a chiffon evening dress and a pair of black satin slippers. They presented them to Nance and told her that it was all arranged for her to go to a public dance with Molly and a party of friends. To Nance it seemed more like an ordeal than a treat. She was almost in tears when Ned took pity on her and persuaded the others to drop the plan. She entered the Ursuline Convent in November and was given the name of Sister Eucharia.

The next to go was Enda in 1933. She had fallen under the spell of Mother Patern, a charismatic Scotswoman who was vocations director for the Franciscan Missionaries of Mary and who in the space of ten years attracted no fewer than fifteen pupils of the Thurles convent to the order. Enda applied for admission to the Franciscan Missionaries and was accepted. She had matriculated the previous year and was due to sit her Leaving Certificate in June, but she was so impatient to join the order that she could not wait that long. She told her parents that she wanted to go to the FMM convent in March without sitting her exam.

Once again Ned was in favour of caution, this time with more reason. Enda at seventeen was a year younger than Nance had been and the break with home would be an even more final one. In the normal course of events, after six months in Loughglynn she would be sent to the novitiate in France and from there to one of the order's missions in Africa or the Far East. She would probably never see her parents, her family, her home or her country again.

Ned's words of caution fell on deaf ears. Enda had made up her mind and was determined to go. He did not want to oppose what now seemed to him to be the will of God and so he withdrew his objections. Enda left the Ursuline school in March and was received into the FMM Convent at Loughglynn in County Roscommon.

Molly watched the departure of her two sisters to the religious life with mixed feelings. While she was happy for them, she could not help thinking of her own ambition, which seemed as far away from fulfilment as ever. Her father's health was continuing to fail and he had become very dependent on his eldest daughter. He now spent every night at home. The family had bought a car which Molly had learnt to drive so that she could bring him round his circuit of fairs and back to Little Island in the evening. She hesitated a long time before she told him what was in her mind. 'Moll, what would I do without you?' he said. She never mentioned the matter again.

During the summer Molly drove her mother and some of the junior members of the family to Loughglynn to visit Enda. Ned was not well and was left at home with Kitty looking after him. They found Enda well and in good spirits. Molly was impressed by Mother Patern and by the atmosphere of the place. It was her first visit to Loughglynn and she found it a memorable one. Her passengers also found it memorable, but for different reasons. Always a somewhat erratic driver, she seemed more than usually abstracted as she drove away from the convent. As she turned out the gate, one of the rear doors of the car swung open and was demolished by the stone gatepost. Molly got out and surveyed the damage. 'It'll all be the same in a hundred years' time', she said.

On 17 September 1934 Enda received the religious habit in Loughglynn and became Sister Fergus. The whole family drove up for the occasion. It was the first time Enda had seen her father in six months and she was shocked at his appearance. He seemed to have suddenly become an old man.

After the ceremony, the family had a meal together in the convent and then they said their goodbyes to Enda who was starting on her journey to France that same day. Ned knew that he would never see her again and seemed completely broken by the parting. Not since the death of little Walburga had his children seen him so grief-stricken. He walked into the woods that surrounded the convent and disappeared from their view, stumbling like a blind man. As the time went by and he failed to return, they began to worry but they hesitated to do anything that would intrude on his sorrow. Almost five hours passed before he came back. He had been walking through the trees in a daze, not knowing where he was going, wrestling with the one problem he had hoped never to have to face again, the loss of a child.

* * *

38

Ned and the family returned to Little Island. Almost immediately another blow fell on them. Nance had been unwell for some time in the Ursuline Convent. Now the news came that tuberculosis had been diagnosed and that she was being sent for treatment to a nursing home in Dublin. The disease of consumption, as it was then called, was widespread among young people in their teens and twenties and often fatal. Ned felt he was being stripped of everything he loved. 'He is playing the will of God with us now', he said.

His own health continued to decline. Spasms of pain became frequent and intense, allied with a distaste for certain forms of food. Then in January 1935 he developed symptoms of jaundice. The doctors told him that he must have an operation for the removal of gall-stones as soon as the jaundice had cleared up.

Before going into hospital for the operation, he travelled to Dublin to see Nance in her nursing-home. It was a strangely emotional encounter. Each thought it was their last meeting because each thought the other was about to die. Ned opened his heart to her as never before. He told her how as a young man he had been sent to bring home his seventeen-year-old sister Rita, dying of consumption in her boarding school in Drogheda. Within six weeks of that sad journey she was dead. Then his beloved sister Annie, who had nursed Rita in those last weeks, was struck down by the same disease and died. Nance describes the effect this had on him in these words:

> For Ned, Annie's death was the climax of a very purifying experience. The shortness of life, the futility of ambitions which can alienate from God, the necessity for Christ's love to be lived out in a total dedication within the framework of one's personal vocation — these were the flames that consumed his soul for months. The experience passed, but henceforth life became very simple.

Listening to him from her hospital bed, Nance understood him better and loved him more than she had ever done before. She also grew in understanding of Molly, the closest to Ned of all the family, who shared his simplicity and transparency. 'Life is for living and Christ is for giving', was a great saying of Ned's. It summed up his character and Molly's too.

On 2 April he was admitted to the Bon Secours Home in Cork and was operated on three days later. When he recovered consciousness, he was found to be paralysed and in great pain. He lingered on for four days. His thoughts were on God and on his family, especially Molly. To a friend who visited him he said, 'If I pull out of this, I'm going to let Moll enter. She has waited too long'. He died on 9 April 1935. He was fifty-nine.

Even though they had been expecting it, the family were devastated by his death. For as long as they could remember, he had been the heart of their home and the centre of their lives. Molly was more deeply affected than any of the others. She went through the funeral in a state of shock, unable even to cry. For the rest of her life, Ned's death was to be the yardstick by which all other human griefs were measured.

It was the ever-practical Nora who forced her to face reality again. Towards the end of April, she tackled Molly about her future and told her that she was now free to enter the convent if she still wanted to. There was nothing any longer to hold her back. Ned was gone, the family were growing up, Nora herself had recovered most of her old health and vigour. Molly was twenty-eight. It was time for her to make up her mind and act.

Molly had to admit the truth of what her mother was saying. She took stock of her situation and found that her desire to be a nun was as strong as ever. It was not that she didn't enjoy life, or that she lacked friends or indeed admirers. One of her admirers, whom we shall call Gerry, had been paying unsuccessful court to her for almost five years. Molly treated him kindly but gave him no encouragement. She pretended not to know that she was the attraction that brought him so often to the house and any time she went out with him she made sure that there were others in the party as well. She liked Gerry and respected him, but neither he nor any other man could fulfil the longing in her heart.

She decided to go to Loughglynn and speak to Mother Patern. The Franciscan Missionaries of Mary had made a deeper impression on her than any other order. They seemed to be making the fullest possible response to the invitation of Christ, 'Go, sell everything you have and then come, follow me'. There were no half-measures about them. They gave everything to God. They held nothing back. She would be glad to be one of them if they would accept her.

Early in May she made the journey to Loughglynn. A friend who accompanied her for part of the way noticed how happy she seemed to be, singing aloud as she drove along. When she arrived at the convent, she met Mother Patern and had a long talk with her. Mother Patern's reaction was not quite as positive as she had expected. The nun pointed out that it was only a month since her father's death and that she was still in a somewhat emotional state. It was not the time for making a decision that would determine all the rest of her life. She asked Molly to go back home, think and pray about the matter, and come back again later in the summer if she was still of the same mind. Molly left, a little crestfallen.

Her friends knew nothing about her plans. To them she was still the same Molly, gradually recovering from her bereavement. She drove the car, she played tennis, she swam, she sang. One of her favourite songs had always been Percy French's *Ach, I dunno*. When she sang it now, it had an irony that her hearers were not aware of:

> I'm simply surrounded by lovers,
> Since Da made his fortune in land;
> They're coming in droves like the plovers
> To ax for me hand.
> There's clerks and policemen and teachers,
> Some sandy, some black as a crow;
> Ma says you get used to the creatures,
> But, ach, I dunno!

> The convent is in a commotion
> To think of me taking a spouse,
> And they wonder I hadn't the notion
> Of taking the vows.
> 'Tis a beautiful life and a quiet
> And keeps you from going below,
> As a girl I thought I might try it,
> But, ach, I dunno!

> I've none but meself to look after,
> And marriage it fills me with fears;
> I think I'd have less of the laughter
> And more of the tears.
> I'll not be a slave like me mother,
> With six of them all in a row,
> Even one little baby's a bother,
> But, ach, I dunno!

There's a lad that has taken me fancy,
I know he's a bit of a limb,
And though marriage is terrible chancy,
I'd chance it with him!
He's coming tonight — oh, I tingle,
From the top of me head to me toe;
I'll tell him I'd rather live single,
But, ach, I dunno!

Molly knew now what she wanted. It was time to pay another visit to Loughglynn. This time her companion was the faithful Gerry, who drove her in his own car. He knew what she was planning to do and he spent the whole journey vainly trying to talk her out of it.

When Mother Patern was faced by the pair of them in the parlour at Loughglynn, she must have thought that Molly had changed her mind. She soon found out the true state of affairs when Gerry renewed his efforts once again. In the nun's presence, he asked Molly if she would agree to become his wife. Molly answered lightly, 'I've brought up one family and I don't intend to bring up another'. It was hardly the full reason but the time for argument was past. It was decided that Molly would enter the convent as a postulant in September and begin her life as a Franciscan Missionary of Mary.

There were a lot of things to be done. There were preparations to be made, clothes to be bought, affairs to be wound up. There were friends to be told and said goodbye to, all of whom would react with the greatest astonishment to the news. But these things would sort themselves out. The important thing was that the dream of a lifetime was about to come true.

She knew the meaning of the decision she was making. It meant that she would leave her home for ever. She would never see it again, not even for a brief visit. Her life would be spent abroad in whatever part of the world the order sent her to.

She would take the three vows of poverty, chastity and obedience. Poverty meant that she would have no possessions of her own but would depend on the order for food, clothing, housing and everything else. Chastity meant that she would give up her right to marriage and family and a home of her own, the sacrifice of all those womanly and motherly feelings that she possessed in such abundance. Obedience meant that she would place herself completely at the disposal of her superiors not only in large matters but also in the smallest actions of her everyday life.

All this she knew in general even if not yet in full detail. Many of the things she had enjoyed doing in the past she would never do again. She would never again dance or swim or play tennis. She would never take part in an opera or musical comedy or even visit a theatre to see one. There would be no more fashionable clothes or shoes or hairstyles. She would be swathed from head to foot in shapeless and voluminous clothing with only her face and hands visible. Everything that made life worth living seemed about to be taken away from her.

Yet not everything. Everything except the one thing that really mattered. Molly was not a complicated person. She saw things in simple terms. She remembered the words of the catechism that she had learnt by heart and never forgotten. 'God made us to know, love and serve him here on earth and to see and enjoy him for ever in heaven.' As a missionary sister, her whole life would be one of adoration, love and service. The things she was giving up were things that had no relevance to that life, things that could distract her from living it to the full. In giving up these lesser loves, she was giving herself to the greater one.

On the way home Molly was bubbling over with happiness. Gerry did not share her feelings. She playfully suggested to him that he might like to give his car as a present to the nuns to help them in their work.

'I offered you everything I have and you refused,' he said. 'The nuns can do without my car.'

5

NOVITIATE

On the morning of 16 September 1935 Molly left her home in Little Island for the six-hour drive to Loughglynn. She was at the wheel of the car with her mother beside her and two of her sisters in the back. She was singing the Easter antiphon *Haec dies* as she drove. 'This is the day the Lord has made: let us rejoice and be glad in it.'

The sun was setting as they reached Loughglynn. Molly negotiated the gate safely and drove up to the main door of the building. In 1903 the Franciscan Missionaries had bought Loughglynn House, a fine Georgian mansion surrounded by gardens and woods and overlooking the lake, Lough Glynn, which gives the district its name. They converted the house to serve as a convent and also as a school of domestic economy where girls from the neighbourhood were trained in carpet-weaving, needlework and butter- and cheese-making.

It was too late for the family to head back for Cork so they stayed the night in Loughglynn. Next morning Molly was given her postulant's dress to wear. She was to spend six months as a postulant before becoming a novice and being allowed to put on the habit of the order. During this period she wore a black veil and ankle-length black dress.

After lunch she said good-bye to the family in the convent parlour. Someone asked her for a last song before parting and suggested *Ach, I dunno*. She seemed a little taken back at first but then she sat down at the piano and sang. At the end of the third verse, she stopped suddenly, evidently feeling that the last verse would not be appropriate to the occasion. After a short pause she launched into another favourite of hers, *The Fairy Tree*.

Then she rose from the piano, saw her mother and sisters off, and began her new life as a Franciscan Missionary of Mary.

The period of postulancy is a period during which the candidate gets to know the order she is joining and the order gets to know the candidate. It gives each an opportunity to judge whether they are likely to get along with the other. The six months' postulancy in Loughglynn was for Molly an introduction to the religious life and especially to the spirit of the order which she hoped to enter as a nun.

One of the first things she learned was that it was not an order and that she was not going to be a nun. Strictly speaking, a religious order is an institute whose members take solemn vows, and it is only women who belong to such orders who are entitled to be called nuns. The Franciscan Missionaries of Mary took simple vows only. Therefore they ranked as a congregation rather than an order, and their members were sisters, not nuns. These technicalities were of interest mainly to canon lawyers; in everyday usage, the FFMs were referred to as nuns or sisters without any sharp distinctions being drawn.

Of far greater importance was her initiation into the spirit and mind of the Franciscan Missionaries of Mary. The congregation was founded in 1877 by Hélène de Chappotin, a dynamic Frenchwoman who had already spent some years in two other religious orders before deciding to start her own. She took the name in religion of Mother Mary of the Passion. Her dynamism and determination swept away all obstacles and attracted vocations in such large numbers that by the time of her death in 1904 the order had eighty-six convents spread throughout Europe, Asia, Africa and America.

The thrust of the congregation was uncompromisingly missionary. The houses in Europe were for the purpose of recruiting and training workers for the missions. The houses in Africa and Asia represented the real purpose of the foundation, which was, as the foundress herself constantly reminded her sisters, the quest for souls.

> My sisters, when I entered your chapel, I was impressed by the painting of the agony of Our Lord which is over the altar. It seemed to me that the Divine Master, with hands outstretched, was calling aloud to us all: 'Souls! Souls!'

I would like you to listen to that call of Jesus and to respond to it. I would like you to be consumed with the burning thirst for souls which consumed him. If until the present you have not been afire with that sacred flame, plunge now into the bottomless abyss, the love of Jesus.

Souls cost Our Lord dearly. He had to drink the cup of suffering to the dregs in order to acquire the title of Saviour. He wants to associate us in his work, to make of us little co-saviours. We must quench our thirst at the same bitter cup.

Be ready for sacrifices, or you will never be missionaries. Love God very much. Plunge into his love with your entire being. Then you will love others too. You will thirst for souls as he did. Oh, comfort him in his thirst! His outstretched hands are pleading!

The austere and single-minded character of her teaching was reflected in the rule which she drew up for her sisters. It made few concessions to human weakness. In this it differed little from other French religious institutes founded during the nineteenth century. They remembered the laxity and corruption of the Church in France in the eighteenth century and how it had led to the virtual collapse of religion during the years of the French Revolution. In reacting against this laxity they were in some danger of going to the opposite extreme.

The three vows of poverty, chastity and obedience were fundamental to all these religious rules. The FMM rule laid special emphasis on poverty, in keeping with its Franciscan spirit. Mother Mary of the Passion also stressed the importance of obedience in a missionary congregation. 'Every Franciscan Missionary of Mary', she wrote, 'promises on the day of her profession that she will always hold herself in readiness to leave her country and her family. She belongs to all and must feel at home wherever love of Our Lord sends her through the voice of obedience.' In regard to prayer, she wanted her sisters to share her devotion to the real presence of Christ in the Eucharist, and she laid down that the Blessed Sacrament should be exposed in the monstrance for adoration every day in each convent.

None of these things presented any problem to Molly in principle. She knew and accepted the three vows. She was prepared to leave her home and her country: there was no other way of being a missionary. She wanted to pray and to learn about prayer, and she had always had a particular devotion to the Blessed Sacrament. The hours of adoration in the convent chapel were a joy rather than a burden and remained so until the end of her life.

It was the smaller details that hurt, the constant pressure of petty customs and regulations. Most of her companions had come to Loughglynn straight from school and even they found the discipline difficult to accept. It was far harder for Molly, twenty-eight years of age, accustomed for the last ten years to being her own boss, running a house and family, driving a car, taking part in sports and theatricals, enjoying life to the full. She now found out that obedience was not just a matter of going to Africa when you were sent. It affected everything you did, what you read, what you ate, the way you talked and walked and laughed — or abstained from laughing.

Laughing was one of the things that caused Molly trouble. Her laugh, infectious and spontaneous, was not regarded as appropriate to convent life. It was undisciplined in itself and was the cause of lack of discipline in others. A nun's laugh should be decorous and refined, as should all her demeanour. Her voice should be low and well-modulated, her gestures restrained, her walk sedate. She should be able to glide noiselessly along the polished floors, opening and closing doors without making a sound.

Then there was custody of the eyes. A nun should never look around her in an idle and inquisitive manner. Her gaze should be directed forward and modestly downcast. This was particularly important in dealing with a member of the opposite sex. In some convents, nuns were recommended to fix their eyes on the general area of a man's collar stud. As an additional safeguard, a nun could never be alone with any outsider apart from her immediate family but must always be accompanied by another nun. Written communications were similarly supervised. Any letter sent or received by a nun had to pass first through the hands of her superior. This applied even to Molly's correspondence with her mother right to the end of her life.

The nun's dress was a further restraint. The length and weight of the habit ruled out any kind of rapid movement and its cut was intended to conceal as much of the occupant as possible. The habit did however retain a certain traditional dignity, based as it was on seventeenth-century peasant dress. The ugly postulant's dress lacked even that dignity. As regards the underwear, it is enough to say that it harked back to an era which valued durability above daintiness. Fortunately, Molly was able to see the funny side. One of her companions recalled her working one day in the laundry and pulling out of the tub an enormous pair of workman's pants. 'I wonder which of the nuns wears these?' she inquired innocently.

Each of these elements, taken separately, could be historically explained and justified. The celibate and community life of its very nature called for certain restraints and safeguards. But the stage had come when these restraints were being valued for themselves rather than for what they protected. In his pioneering book, *The Nun in the World*, Cardinal Suenens said in public what many had been thinking in private and made a powerful plea for a style of religious life that would respond to the needs of the modern world.

> Physical and psychological detachment from the world leads a religious to turn in on herself and her own community. Her world shrinks and if she is not careful will end up no more than a few square yards in size. Whence comes distorted vision, seeing everything from one angle, measuring things against a diminished scale. Whence, again, the contrived and artificial nature of certain customs in religious houses — a sort of 'house etiquette', a stilted, stereotyped and unnatural behaviour. It has been said of certain congregations of nuns that they are 'the last strongholds of the very studied manners of the middle-class woman of the nineteenth century.' People would like to see more spontaneity, less inhibition, more natural and straightforward reactions.

The Suenens book was published in 1962 on the eve of the Second Vatican Council. After the Council a thorough reform of religious rules and customs was undertaken. By that time Molly was dead.

* * *

The fact that Molly lasted out her six months in Loughglynn was due to a number of factors. Apart from the grace of God, there was Molly's own character — humble, cheerful, prayerful, and with the strength that comes from simplicity. It was not for her to question the traditions of the order, no matter how irksome some of them might seem. It was God's will that she should endure them for the sake of a greater good. She came across a saying that she found very consoling: 'God writes straight with crooked lines.' What appeared to her meaningless must somehow be part of the divine plan.

In all this she was greatly helped by the wisdom and gentleness of Mother Patern, who was adept at tempering the wind to the shorn lamb. Between her and Molly there grew up a real understanding and affection.

Even so, it was a hard struggle. In mid-November, Mother Patern started planning the music for the midnight Mass at Christmas. She asked Molly if she would like to sing some solos. 'Solos, Mother?' she answered. 'You don't think I'm going to be here for midnight Mass, do you? I'll be singing the solos in Glounthane as usual.' Wisely, Mother Patern did not pursue the matter any further.

All the same, the rumour went around the convent that Molly was leaving. Mother Sabas was preparing a concert for the girls in the workroom and had cast Molly as the leading singer. She appeared one day in the kitchen to consult Sister Bridget, the cook. Should she advance the date of the concert in view of the fact that Molly was not likely to be with them much longer? Sister Bridget told her there was no need to worry. Molly had been helping her in the kitchen and she had come to know her well. She had no doubt that she was going to stay.

Christmas came and Molly was still there. She sang the solos at midnight Mass with a radiance and a joy that touched all the congregation. At the concert on Christmas night, she was in sparkling form, singing song after song with infectious enthusiasm. 'This one is going to lift you off your chairs', she promised, as she launched into her final number, *The Kerry Dances*. And it very nearly did.

Whatever the nature of the crisis, it seemed to have been overcome. With the coming of the New Year, Molly showed a new serenity and certainty. The fact that she was ten years older than the other postulants became an advantage rather than a disadvantage. They came to her for advice and support in their own times of crisis. Mother Patern encouraged this trend. One of them remembers being told by her, 'If you have a problem you don't want to discuss with your superior, ask Molly about it.'

One of the postulants who entered with Molly was an only girl, the daughter of wealthy parents. Her mother did everything she could to dissuade her and presented her with one suitor after another, each one more eligible than the last. But the daughter remained unmoved and at length obtained her mother's reluctant consent to enter the convent. She was only a few months there when another suitor, the most eligible of all, came knocking at the mother's door. This was an offer that could not be refused. The mother set off at once for Loughglynn and stormed up the steps to the hall door. 'I've come to take her home', she announced to the startled portress.

Mother Patern was summoned but her most reasoned arguments failed to make any impression. She decided to send for Molly, who had met the mother on an earlier occasion and knew the kind of person she was dealing with. She arrived and went straight to the point.

'What's this I hear?' she said. 'You've come to take her from the Man Above? Tell me, what's so wonderful about this Mr What's-his-name that you think it would be a good exchange?'

She had said all that was needed. She had cut through the arguments to the essence of the matter and touched the deep spring of faith in the mother's heart. She went off home again, happy to leave her daughter in the care of the Man Above.

Molly's six months of postulancy ended in March. There were no longer any doubts on either side. She wanted more than ever to be a Franciscan Missionary of Mary and they were happy to welcome her into their ranks. She was now to be clothed in the habit of the order and to receive a new name, symbolising a new life-style. She asked to be allowed to take the name Eamonn, the Irish form of Edward, her father's name.

The family turned up in force for the ceremony of clothing. They were accompanied by the ever-constant Gerry, come to say a last good-bye. As the choir sang *'Veni, Sponsa Christi'* (Come, Bride of Christ), the postulants entered the convent chapel in solemn procession. Each of them was dressed in the white veil and dress of a bride and carried a bouquet of flowers. The priest took as the text for his sermon the words of St John's Gospel:

'You have not chosen me but I have chosen you, that you should go and bear fruit and that your fruit should remain.' Then Molly and the others withdrew for a few minutes and returned dressed in their religious habit. They knelt in front of the priest as he blessed them and placed crowns of roses on their heads.

The following day she left for the novitiate in France. Before she went, she said goodbye to her family and friends, none of whom she would ever see again. The only one who did not share in the goodbyes was her mother. Nora announced that she intended to travel to France for Enda's profession in six months' time, when she would have an opportunity of seeing Molly once again.

Then she got into the car that would take her to Dublin and the boat for England. The community stood on the steps of the convent singing the mission hymn of the order as she drove away. There was a last glimpse of the old house and the gardens and the yellow carpet of spring daffodils that stretched all the way down to the shores of the lake.

* * *

The central novitiate of the congregation was at a place called Les Châtelets-sous-Bois, not far from the town of St Brieuc on the north coast of Brittany. The old house had been a summer residence of the Bishop of St Brieuc in the palmy days of the Old Regime. It was lost during the French Revolution but was bought back by the Church in 1880 to become the head house and novitiate of the newly-founded Franciscan Missionaries of Mary.

Molly's first months in the novitiate should have been happy ones. Her homesickness could be forgotten in the joy of meeting again her sister Enda, now known as Sister Fergus, who had another six months to spend there before finishing her noviceship. As its name implies, Les Châtelets-sous-Bois is surrounded by acres of woodlands. She could look forward to pleasant afternoons wandering through the woods with her sister while the spring days lengthened and ripened into summer.

It was not to be. On the journey from Ireland to France Molly managed to catch a cold. It got worse after she arrived in Les Châtelets and within three weeks she had started to cough blood. The doctor was sent for and she was ordered to the infirmary for a period of complete rest.

Molly said nothing about her illness in her first letters home. There were restrictions on the number of letters she could write. In the novitiate she was allowed to write only one letter a month, and none at all during Lent and Advent. She was allowed to receive as many as were sent to her. Her first letter to Little Island was a plea for plenty of letters and plenty of news from home. 'Keep on writing. Tell all those who promised to write to us we may be nuns but we're not dead. So write even though we can't answer them.' Nora kept this letter and every other letter she got from her until Molly's death thirty years later.

The doctor refused to tell her what the trouble was. He said this could only be decided by an X-ray and she was too weak as yet to travel to the hospital. So she lay in bed while her imagination painted increasingly gloomy pictures of what her future might be. Every young person of the time knew that coughing blood was the first symptom of tuberculosis. It was a disease that had taken its toll of her family. It had killed two of her father's sisters and had threatened to kill her own sister Nance, though she was now happily recovered. It seemed as if her missionary career was to end before it had even begun.

During this time her great consolation was the companionship of her sister Enda, who visited her every day in the infirmary. They decided at length that Enda should write to Nora and break the news about Molly's sickness. Then Molly herself wrote, trying to sound more cheerful than she felt:

I expect you were very surprised when you got Enda's letter to say I was ill. Well, I am feeling a lot better, T.G. The doctor examined me and could not find anything wrong with me. He said I was probably tired from singing. His orders were: Don't cough, talk, laugh or sing — rather a tall order but it has to be done — and to stay in bed for a week. Next morning after his visit I spat some more. After a few days he came again, and again examined me with the same result and the same instructions: only to eat and sleep.

I could not tell you how kind everybody here has been to me. Now I'm nearly a fortnight on the invalids' list. As yet I have not been X-rayed. Say a few prayers that it is not anything serious, as you know what that would mean. But whatever way it goes, it is the Lord's holy will, and we will have to be satisfied. As Dad, RIP, used say, 'How fond of us He is, He never forgets to send us the cross. His holy will be done.'

Ten days later she wrote again. She must have got special permission to write with the good news. 'Thanks be to God and Our Lady. I was X-rayed this morning and everything is absolutely alright. The blood was from my throat, therefore I can't sing for a while yet. But I'm singing a song of thanksgiving in my heart to the Sacred Heart.'

Afterwards Molly made light of the whole episode. 'In the convent you're well looked after when you're sick', she told a companion. 'At home, you have to do your work however bad you feel. I often had a splitting headache and had to stand over a tub of washing just the same.' But she admitted that there had been times when she hoped that her illness would force her superiors to send her back to Ireland. If they had done so, it would have been God's will for her: but she would not force his will by asking for it.

Enda's profession took place in September and Nora travelled to Les Châtelets for the ceremony as she had promised. It was a happy re-union for the three of them. The doctor had told Molly that she must rest her lungs for some time after her illness and had warned her particularly against singing. 'No singing for six months', he said. These warnings were forgotten or ignored in the excitement of the occasion. Molly sang some of the old favourites to a new and largely French-speaking audience. The language barrier did not prevent them from enjoying her songs, especially *The Fairy Tree*, an Irish ballad which tells of a haunted thorn-tree where 'the blessed Son of Mary' once appeared. 'I can't understand a word of English,' said the mistress of novices, 'but Sister Eamonn has such expression in her eyes that I can understand everything she is singing.'

The happiness of these days together made the separation all the harder to bear. Enda had been appointed to Liberia in West Africa and she set off to begin her life as a missionary. Nora returned to Ireland. The parting from Enda was final but there was at least a possibility that Nora would return to Les Châtelets for Molly's own profession in eighteen months' time.

It was lonely after they had gone. There were over a hundred novices in Les Châtelets, the majority of them French. The language of instruction in class and of everyday conversation was French. There were enough Irish there to form an English-speaking group but to prevent this happening the novices were divided into recreation groups of mixed nationalities. There was a reason for this. It avoided the formation of different language cliques in the novitiate and it ensured that non-French speakers would become fluent in French. Their mission assignments would be to convents of mixed nationalities where the common language was French. The novitiate was the place to prepare them for this.

For the rest of her life, French was to be Molly's normal means of communication. She found it very difficult at first. In later years, she singled out the language problem as the greatest single trial she had to undergo in the novitiate. For someone so naturally outgoing, the inability to communicate was hard to bear. It also cut her off from news of the outside world. The novices were not allowed newspapers and their knowledge of current events came by word of mouth. It took months before Molly discovered exactly why they were being asked to pray for their nuns in Spain. Eventually she became as fluent speaking in French as in English, but her grasp of the grammar was always a little unsure and showed itself in her writing.

Daily life in the novitiate was a combination of physical work, study and prayer. The work included washing, cleaning, polishing, cooking, gardening, and various jobs around the farm, none of which caused Molly any trouble. The study covered theology, scripture, spirituality and Church history. Enda had been given the task of lecturing the English-speaking novices in history and by some process of heredity it was passed on to Molly. She found that the best way of learning a subject is by teaching it. Her study of the Reformation in England convinced her of the danger of trying to set up a national church. When she found herself facing a similar situation in China, she had no doubts about what her attitude should be.

Prayer was her greatest source of strength and consolation. The order's devotion to the Blessed Sacrament was one of the things that had attracted her. She loved to kneel in adoration before the monstrance in the high-vaulted convent chapel. She sent home a glowing account of the outdoor procession on the Feast of Corpus Christi, winding its way through the grounds from one altar to another, along walks that had been turned into carpets by intricate designs of flowers and moss. At each altar there was Benediction and at each Benediction she prayed for the intentions of all her family.

The little pin-pricks of convent life continued. When she was happy, Molly liked to sing. She was happy now. In the sewing-room, where the novices spent much of their time making and mending for the community and for the missions, silence was supposed to be observed. Molly was reported to her superior for breaking the silence by humming to herself as she worked, and the superior reported her to the provincial. However, the provincial did not take too serious a view of the matter. She told Molly she could sing away at her work as long as she avoided disturbing others.

The winter of 1937/38 was a severe one in Brittany. Molly was working in the farm-yard and had difficulty getting through the deep snow, wearing wooden sabots in place of the familiar rubber boots. Then cheering news came from Ireland. In spite of the weather, her mother had decided to come to her profession, which was scheduled for 19 March. Molly sent a delighted letter to Little Island, full of instruction and advice about the journey. Nora was to stay in St Brieuc and not to come to the convent until the 19th, as Molly would be on retreat. After the ceremony, she could stay for a few days until Molly left for her mission assignment. Where that would be, she had as yet not the faintest idea.

Nora made the journey safely and was in her place in the convent chapel on the 19th, the Feast of St Joseph, patron saint of Les Châtelets. She caught her first glimpse of Molly in eighteen months when the forty novices who were to be professed walked in procession up the centre aisle to the high altar. They were greeted by the presiding bishop, who then put to them the traditional questions of the profession ceremony:

> 'Will you take Jesus Christ, Son of God most High, as your spouse forever?'
> 'Yes, I will, and desire to do so with all my heart.'
> 'Will you keep the vows of obedience, poverty and chastity according to the constitutions of the Institute?'
> 'Yes, I will, with the help of God.'
> 'Will you follow unto death Jesus crucified, in imitating his most pure Mother and your seraphic father St Francis, offering yourself as a victim for the Church and the salvation of souls?'

'Yes, I will, with the help of God.'

'Will you consecrate yourself for ever to the missions of the Sacred Congregation for the Propagation of the Faith in accordance with holy obedience?'

'Yes, I will, with the help of God.'

A veil, a ring and a crown of thorns were blessed by the bishop for each of the candidates. The prayers of blessing explained the meaning of each of these. The veil was a sign of consecration to the service of God and his Church. The ring symbolised betrothal to Christ as his spouse in chastity and fidelity. The thorns were a reminder that those who would share in the work of Christ must also be prepared to share in his suffering. As the bishop placed the crown of thorns on the candidate's head he said: 'Receive this crown which your celestial spouse offers you, that you may be worthy to participate in his passion on earth and his glory in heaven.' Then the candidates pronounced their three vows of poverty, chastity and obedience. The ceremony ended with the singing of the *Te Deum*, the Church's solemn hymn of thanksgiving.

They had entered the chapel as novices. They left as Franciscan Missionaries of Mary. The vows they had taken were temporary vows, to be renewed annually; only after another three years would they make their final profession and take perpetual vows. By that time many of them would be seasoned missionaries, working in whichever corner of the world their superiors had sent them to.

Of the forty newly-professed, the majority were assigned to further studies. Only two were to go immediately to the missions. One was to go to Morocco. The other, Molly, was to go to China.

6

VOYAGE TO THE EAST

China had a special place in the annals of the Franciscan Missionaries of Mary. They had over fifty convents there, more than in any other country in the world. It had been the scene of their greatest triumphs and their greatest tragedies.

Their first convent in China was founded in Chefoo in the year 1886. From there they pushed deep into the interior of the country, travelling by river-steamers and native junks, walking through mountain passes and valleys, setting up convents and schools and hospitals in places where no European woman had ever been seen before. The risks they faced were very real. As well as the ever-present dangers of famine and flood and disease, they had to contend with the people's deep suspicion of all foreigners, which could erupt into violence at any time. They were soon made painfully aware of this. The convent in Ichang, founded in 1889, was attacked by an angry mob shortly afterwards and burnt to the ground. The nuns barely escaped with their lives.

The Boxer rising of 1900 brought matters to a head. The Boxers were a secret society who believed, not without reason, that the European powers were exploiting the weakness of China for their own selfish ends. A series of uprisings took place all over the vast Chinese empire with the aim of destroying the foreign devils and restoring China to her ancient greatness.

The European embassies in Peking, guarded by troops and artillery, barely managed to survive an eight-week siege. The defenceless missionaries scattered throughout the countryside could only flee or go into hiding. Many were caught and put to death, often after appalling tortures. One of the worst massacres took place in Taiyuanfu, where all the missionaries of the locality, both Catholic and Protestant, were rounded up and imprisoned. On 9 July 1900 they were brought before the governor of the town. Without even the formality of a trial, he sentenced them to death. The executions took place immediately. Among those who died were seven women, Franciscan Missionaries of Mary who had come to the town the previous year and set up a home for orphan girls.

The death of the seven nuns made a profound impression on the FMM congregation. It was at once a sadness and a joy. They were the first martyrs of the congregation and their blood cemented its commitment to the Chinese mission. There is an old saying that the blood of martyrs is the seed of Christians. The thousands of Christians, natives as well as foreigners, who died during the Boxer rising, helped to strengthen and purify the Church in China after peace had been restored. The death of the seven nuns inspired many young women in Europe to enter the order to which they had belonged.

From the time of her profession, Molly was officially known as Mother Mary of St Eamonn, or Mother Eamonn for short. (In recent years, the use of the title Mother has been dropped and all the nuns are now called Sister, apart from the Mother General.) A week after the ceremony, Nora said goodbye to her daughter and returned to Ireland. It was the last and saddest of the partings. They knew they would never see one another again. Nora's last words to her were, ' 'Tis not he who can inflict most but he who can endure most is the victor'. Molly never forgot those words and they were to be a source of strength to her during her long years of trial in Peking.

Molly did not have time to brood over the pain of that parting. There were too many preparations that had to be made for the long journey to her new home. In a way it seemed that everything that had happened to her up to this had been a preparation. Now at last her real life was about to begin.

The packing did not take long. She had practically nothing in the way of personal belongings. Europeans travelling to the Far East normally brought mountains of luggage. The sisters brought only a change of clothing and a few books for themselves. Most of their luggage consisted of items for the convents in China which could only be obtained in Europe: chalices, statues, crucifixes, medals, rosaries, music, liturgical books and the like.

Molly's instructions were to go to Paris and from there to Marseilles in the south of France, where she would catch the boat for Shanghai. In Shanghai she would be assigned by the local superior to one of the Chinese convents. But when she arrived in Paris she found that there had been a welcome change of plan. The ship she was to take, the *Conte Rosso*, was leaving from Brindisi in the south of Italy. This meant that she would be able to visit Rome and pray at the tombs of the apostles. Above all, she would be able to see the Pope and receive his blessing.

In these days of cheap and easy air travel for both Popes and pilgrims, such happenings are commonplace. For Molly it was literally a once-in-a-lifetime experience. She wrote from Paris with the news, 'When you tell Enda I am in Rome, I can hear her saying, "She's got away with it again." Really, that's how I feel this time myself. I had not a notion or a hope of going to Rome. The Lord is really very good to me.'

In Rome she stayed at the head house of the order in the Via Giusti. She crammed every minute of every day with sight-seeing. She wrote home long and enthusiastic descriptions of all the churches she had visited and all the relics she had seen, however improbable some of them might have been:

> We started with the Basilica of the Holy Cross of Jerusalem. In the chapel there is a great big piece of the good thief's cross, the inscription of Our Lord's cross, St Thomas's finger, one of the nails of Our Lord, a piece of the column at which Our Lord was scourged. And then we mounted the Holy Stairs at the top of which is a chapel which women are not allowed to enter in which there are several relics of Our Lord, also a painting of Our Lord by St Luke which was finished by the angels.

The highlight of her stay in Rome was her visit to the Vatican for an audience with Pope Pius XI.

> It was an audience for the newly-wed(!) and we had admission tickets. One of our Mothers came with us. Her brother is a noble at the court of the Holy Father and she got us a little gallery very near the Pope. We had to wait a while and then he arrived on a chair supported by eight pages. He began to speak when he was on the throne. He spoke in Italian and it was translated for us. He said that

he blessed us, all that was in our hearts, all our families, and every enterprise dear to our own hearts and those of whom we loved. So I'd say every one of you had the Pope's blessing.

On the very night before she left Rome for the boat at Brindisi, a dramatic little incident occurred. She did not mention it in any of her letters at the time, no doubt to avoid causing anxiety to her family. News arrived at the head house that three of their nuns had been killed in Chanloo in China. The Mother General sent for Molly and the other sisters who were about to leave for China and told them that in view of the situation there they were free to stay in Europe if they wished. Molly and the others all decided to go ahead. The memory of that decision stayed with her and she was to recall it when a similar situation arose ten years later.

On the way to Brindisi next day, her farmer's eye noted the poverty of the land. 'Each little house on the mountain has its little bit of cultivated ground, but how hard it has been to cultivate it God only knows.' In Brindisi she and the sisters travelling with her boarded the *Conte Rosso*, bound for Shanghai via the Mediterranean, the Suez Canal and the Indian Ocean. It was a ship often used by missionaries travelling to the Far East. Five years earlier, it had brought St Maximilian Kolbe on one of his journeys to Japan. The presence of priests on board meant that the sisters could attend Mass and receive Communion each morning.

On the voyage Molly kept a journal of the places she visited and the sights she saw. After a quick journey through the eastern Mediterranean, the ship passed through Port Said into the Suez Canal. It was Molly's first experience of tropical heat and of life in what is now called the Third World. She was not very favourably impressed by either.

The heat in the canal was intense, especially for someone wearing the robes and headdress of a nun. Molly had always had a tendency to plumpness, kept at bay through regular exercise. Since entering the convent, she no longer had the opportunity to swim or play tennis and she began steadily putting on weight. It was to remain a problem for the rest of her life, though not one that she worried about too much. But it did make life uncomfortable in the heat of an Egyptian spring or a Chinese summer.

From the deck of the *Conte Rosso*, Molly had her first glimpse of the way the people of the Third World lived. In the Suez Canal she saw boatloads of stone being pulled along by men tied together like pack animals. In the Eritrean port of Massawah she watched the native dockers at work and remembered what Enda had said in her letters from West Africa.

> If you saw those unfortunate men last night unloading the boat! Their tunics were opened in front, you could see their hearts beating with exertion. And they being driven by the white men as if they were beasts. I know now why they are feared and dreaded by the blacks. Like Enda, I'd say the white man is over-civilised.

The ship docked at Bombay, where the FMMs had two convents. One of the nuns ended her journey there and the others disembarked for a few hours to see the city. All the shop signs were in English and the people in the streets spoke English. Were it not for the dark faces, the nuns could have imagined they were in England. They passed a little church packed to the door with Indians hearing Mass but were deterred from entering by the heat which was, if anything, worse than in the Red Sea. Molly found herself in a constant lather of perspiration. Then they rejoined the ship for the next leg of the journey, to Colombo in Ceylon.

> We went ashore at Colombo as we have a large general hospital, a house in the poorer part of the town, an orphanage, a babies' hostel, and outside in the country a novitiate for the Indians. The novitiate is lovely, open and airy. It is lovely to see the coloured sisters just the same as us. No distinction between the coloured race and us in our houses. It is really Our Lord's teaching put into practice. Love one another as I have loved you.

There was a further stop at Singapore. Molly was enchanted by the long approach to the port from the sea, so different from the sudden descent of the modern air traveller.

> I never saw anything so beautiful as the entrance and exit to the harbour; you enter between chains of islands, on both sides of which the tropical vegetation descends into the waters; the earth, when you get a glimpse of it, is red and the grass a bright green. It is a reflex of heaven, all these

islands surrounded by a sea vividly blue. I felt like singing the *Te Deum* as we sang it once on the lakes of Killarney. To see all that beauty at once, and it's only earthly beauty: what is the beauty of heaven like? It certainly is worth fighting a few years for it.

The port is of course an English one, and it is written all over it. Beside the boat there were divers in little skiffs, who dived in the water to gather the money the passengers threw to them. I think their normal trade is pearl fishing. Their little boats were like cockle shells which they left to the winds and weather to dive.

Their last stop before Shanghai was at Hong Kong. Though a British colony, Hong Kong was geographically part of China and its inhabitants were nearly all Chinese. Along the waterfront Molly saw many sights that saddened her. They brought home to her very painfully the poverty of the country and the war that was beginning to tear her apart. The previous year, the Japanese had taken advantage of the chaotic state of China to launch an invasion from the north. They had already occupied a large area of the country, including the cities of Peking, Tientsin and Shanghai.

This morning we got stuck in a dock yard to unload goods and beside us was a destroyer. She had two aeroplanes on her deck and several cannons. The look of her would give you the creeps. What will it be like to hear her guns roaring? Two of our Mothers from a neighbouring town came to see us and said the war was in the interior of China now. It's funny, I'm not a bit upset whether it is war or no. I'm here by obedience and am perfectly sure I'm doing the will of God — so it's his job to protect us while we do his work of charity.

In stark contrast to the warship were the pathetic floating homes of the boat-dwellers, which filled every available space in the harbour. 'Not the most beautiful way of living,' noted Molly.

How they exist is a puzzle. There are sixty million of them who live on the water. They are born on the water, live and die on the water. It is these who are swept away during the typhoon and all the other climatic miseries of the East.

Molly as a young girl.

Molly (right) with her sister, Kitty.

Molly (centre) with her brother, Eamonn and sister, Enda (1930).

Molly in 'The Gondoliers'

The chapel at Les Châtelets.

Sister Eamonn's final profession at Peking.

The front steps of the Sacred Heart Convent, Peking.

Superintendent Matt O'Sullivan of the Hong Kong Police, on duty at Lo Wu Railway Station.

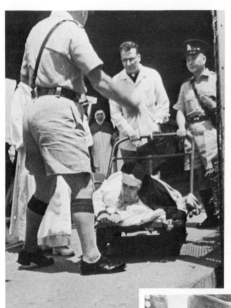

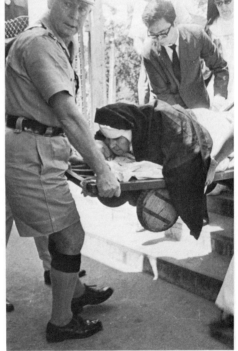

Molly's journey to freedom,
over the bridge at Lo Wu.

The burial in Hong Kong.

Molly's remains arrive at Cork Airport. Her mother (centre) and sisters Pam (left) and Nance.

Thousands of them each year are killed like that — and each one of them cost the blood of Our Lord. Our Mothers yesterday asked why are there not more missionaries coming out to save those souls who are crying out to be saved.

The short journey from Hong Kong to Shanghai proved unexpectedly eventful. The ship ran into dense fog and struck a rock. There was a danger that the passengers might have to abandon ship and take to the lifeboats but the crew managed to contain the damage and let the ship proceed. After about half an hour of slow travel they almost ran into a Chinese trawler and the captain decided it would be more prudent to stay where he was until the fog lifted. It was three days before the ship could start moving again. 'I've a notion she is shipping a lot of water, we are going so slowly,' Molly noted, 'but with God's help we will arrive soon at Shanghai.'

On the night of 31 May, 1938, the *Conte Rosso* limped into Shanghai. After three weeks on the ocean, Molly was now at last in China, even if this part was under Japanese control. She found herself in a city at war, its population swollen by thousands of refugees. The FMMs were working night and day, trying to feed and shelter the homeless and nurse the wounded. In addition to the two hospitals they had been running, another two had now been put into their charge.

In Shanghai, Molly was told that she was being assigned to the northern province of the congregation. She took to the sea again with two other sisters, bound for the city of Tientsin. This time she travelled on a creaky old tramp steamer, very different from the ocean-going liner that had brought her from Europe.

The first thing that struck me on the boat was that one end was like an iron cage and there were four men fully armed walking up and down the deck. They were four Russian guards to protect us from pirates. Sometimes when they are out at sea, the third class passengers become pirates and there is a first class battle. But this time it passed off all right.

Even if the third class passengers managed to refrain from acts of piracy, the voyage was not a pleasant one. The small boat pitched and rolled and the other two sisters were sea-sick, though

Molly escaped. Then a baby on board died of cholera and all the passengers were inspected for symptoms of the disease. Fortunately the three sisters had been inoculated before leaving Shanghai. What Molly found hardest to bear was that there was no priest on board the boat and therefore no Mass and no Blessed Sacrament. 'It was the longest five days I ever spent. But the joy of seeing a monstrance again was heavenly. Whether it's the north of China or Cork, he is always the same and he never lets us down.'

In Tientsin, Molly stayed at the Convent of Our Lady of Victories which was the province's head house and had a famous school attached. She thought at first that she might be kept there, as her proficiency in music and her command of English made her suitable for a teaching post. The superior for some unknown reason — perhaps it was meant as a joke? — decided to give her a new name. 'Rev Mother Superior has changed my name. She calls me Mother Patrick. There is no other Mother Patrick in the province and I look so Irish. Paddy is written all over me.' Whatever the reason, she soon reverted to Eamonn again.

She did not have long to wait for her assignment. She was told that she was to be a teacher, but not in Tientsin. She was to join the community at the Sacred Heart Convent in Peking. Obediently, she set off again on the short train journey inland to the ancient capital of China, now under Japanese occupation like Tientsin and Shanghai. On 20 July 1938, she arrived at the convent that was to be her home for the rest of her life. 'Here I'll stay', she wrote home. 'I've done enough travelling for the next forty years.'

7

THE JAPANESE OCCUPATION

The Sacred Heart Convent was an impressive structure, built in the European style. It was three storeys high — four, if you count the basement — and it towered above the huddle of small houses that surrounded it on all sides. There was an imposing façade, with a wide flight of steps leading up to the pillared portico and main entrance. Above the entrance was a large stone statue of the Sacred Heart.

The community was an interesting mixture of races and languages. Chinese sisters were the single largest group but the common language of communication was French and the mother superior was always a European. The mixture seemed to work well. Even within the same order, some convents can be happier places to live in than others. The Sacred Heart Convent in Peking had a good reputation among the Franciscan Missionaries of Mary for its spirit of prayer and fellowship and for its hospitality to visiting sisters and priests. On the other hand, the rules were applied in a notably rigid manner and Molly found this oppressive. There were times when her relations with her superior became distinctly strained.

When Molly arrived the school was closed for the summer holidays and she spent her first few weeks finding her way around the large convent, getting to know the other members of the community and making an occasional foray into the streets and public gardens of the city, always in company with another sister as the rule demanded. Her first impressions were favourable.

> Peking is very very pretty. The Chinese houses are only one storey high and looking from my window the city looks like a great big forest. All that rise above the trees are the

Emperor's palaces which are painted red with bright yellow roofs. The Chinese are very artistic and everything is decorated, but not much decoration on themselves. Men and women wear a kind of long dress, straight down and tight-fitting, which opens up the side, and a pair of trousers.

The city was at peace under the Japanese army of occupation. For the previous twenty years, Peking had lived from crisis to crisis. The central government had collapsed and most of China was divided among rival generals, the so-called warlords. Each had his own army and territory, each ruled his fiefdom with a mixture of cruelty and corruption and at the same time tried to extend his boundaries at the expense of his neighbour's. Five or six different warlords had ruled Peking in a dozen years and the spectacle of conquering armies entering the city in triumph had become monotonously familiar.

The Japanese were no worse than any of the others. True, they were foreigners and their rule was autocratic and often cruel. But they were no more cruel than the warlords and considerably less corrupt, and they provided stability and a kind of peace. For this reason their rule in Peking was not as much resented by the people as one might have expected. This may be why the city was spared the kind of barbarities which the Japanese forces inflicted on other parts of south-east Asia.

In the eyes of the Christians and many others, the Japanese had the additional virtue of being implacably opposed to Communism. Even in her first surviving letter from Peking, Molly is worried about the activities of Communist guerrillas in the areas where the Japanese were not in full control.

> Whole villages are being evacuated, leaving the place free for the Reds. The very name of a Catholic is enough for them. Three of our nuns have been killed in the south this year and several priests. Last week the Apostolic Delegate came to see us. He told us there are eight to ten thousand orphans in each of the big towns on account of the war. And there is no one to take care of them. 'The harvest indeed is ready but the labourers are few.' Our nuns are doing all they can but they have neither money nor personnel to cope with that amount.

In her next letter, she returns to the same subject. Nuns visiting the house in Peking had given her further information about life in the areas where the Communists were active.

> The place is alive with Reds. We had a superior here last week, and her whole convent, children, old men, women and all, had to go to the priests' residence and remain there several weeks. It would be an easy thing to be killed: there are worse things than death. These barbarians are hopping it with young girls and women, and the fact that our nuns are Europeans makes them more desirable. So they have to either have the priests staying in the house with them, or go and live in the house with the priests for protection.
>
> We had a visitor from another house also. Every day they have to buy seven or eight babies. They have a hundred and twenty in the nursery, all from a month to twelve months old. 30 cents must be paid to the father for each baby, otherwise he would give it to the dogs. They keep three or four children, and every one that arrives after that is given to the nuns to rear.

Meanwhile, Molly was settling down to the daily routine of life in the Sacred Heart Convent. The school had re-opened in September after the summer holidays and she had been assigned her teaching duties. Her main subjects were to be English and music. Most of the pupils were girls, but boys were admitted to the junior classes. There were in fact two schools there, one for Chinese and the other for Europeans. The Chinese school had some 400 pupils on its rolls, and all subjects were taught through the medium of Chinese, mainly by Chinese sisters. The European school catered principally for children of Peking's large foreign community and the teaching was given by European sisters in English or French. Among her pupils Molly counted Chinese, Japanese, Chinese-French, French, Russians, and various combinations of these. 'I'm terrified to ask what nationality they are, because every time I get a shock. No fear of meeting an Irish person here.'

The variety of languages used was a problem for Molly and remained so to the end. It is a surprising fact that in her twenty-eight years in China she never learnt to speak or read more than a few words of Chinese. She might have succeeded in mastering the language if she had begun to study it immediately on arrival but an unexpected complication arose. An order was issued by the Japanese authorities to the effect that from 1940 the medium of instruction in all schools must be Japanese. So Molly started to learn Japanese rather than Chinese. It appears that the order was not rigidly enforced and Molly eventually gave up the attempt to learn the language. By then, however, she had got used to managing in English and French. The effort to learn Chinese, a language reputed to be even more difficult than Japanese for a westerner, hardly seemed worth it.

Behind these reasons was another more fundamental one. It was a question of the attitudes of the missionaries of the period. They brought with them into the countries of Africa and Asia not only their religion but their culture too. They turned their converts not just into Christians but into European Christians. Everything about their new religion was western. The churches they attended were built in gothic or romanesque style. The language in which they worshipped was Latin. The missionaries were prepared to learn the local language if that was the only way of communicating with the natives. But if the natives could be taught to understand French or English, so much the better.

There might be something to be said in favour of this approach when dealing with a primitive tribe in New Guinea or equatorial Africa. But the missionaries in China were confronted with a culture and a civilisation that was far more ancient and venerable than anything Europe had to offer. This fact was recognised in the seventeenth century by the great Jesuit missionary Matteo Ricci, who was for many years the honoured guest and scientific adviser of the Chinese Emperor in Peking. Ricci incorporated into Christianity a number of Chinese elements, including the traditional names for God and heaven and the custom of venerating dead ancestors. After his death, these so-called 'Chinese Rites' were condemned by Rome as reflecting pagan ideas and the condemnation remained in force until the Second Vatican Council.

Whatever the theological rights and wrongs of the controversy, it cannot be doubted that the condemnation of the Chinese Rites helped to make Christianity seem an alien religion to the people. It made it easy for generations of Chinese nationalists to stir up hatred against the missionaries. Their white faces, their strange clothing, their incomprehensible languages and customs, all marked them out as foreign devils. The surprising thing is that in the face of these obstacles, the Christian religion made so much progress in China, especially in the years immediately before the Communist take-over.

In her failure to learn Chinese, Molly was the innocent prisoner of a tradition that she never even thought of questioning. But she may have wondered in those first years in Peking whether this was what she became a nun for. She had dreamed of preaching the Gospel, tending the sick, sheltering the homeless, bringing the healing power of Christ's love to a wounded world. Now she found herself sitting in a classroom in a fashionable school, teaching English grammar to the children of well-to-do Europeans. She never speaks of it in these terms in her letters. But a note of envy creeps in when she refers to Enda and her black babies in Africa or to her fellow FMMs in the Chinese interior, coping with famine and floods and ministering to orphans and refugees.

An unfortunate clash between Molly and her Mother Superior about this time added to her troubles. The mounting tension in Europe was having its effect on the community in Peking. Sisters from opposing nations were getting newspapers from home filled with atrocity stories and other propaganda and these added to the tension. When war finally broke out, the superior decided that it would be in the interests of harmony if she confiscated all newspapers from the belligerent countries immediately upon arrival. Ireland was neutral, so Molly presumed that she would be allowed to receive the papers which her mother sent her regularly, usually enclosing a letter as well.

When her supply of mail began to dry up, Molly became suspicious. She then discovered that her Irish papers were being used to light the fires in the convent and that the letters enclosed in them were not being given to her. In spite of her protests, this continued for some time until Molly got word to her mother to send no more papers but letters only.

The bitterness caused by this incident stayed with Molly for a long time. But she was mature enough to recognise that the cross which has to be carried by every disciple can take many different forms. She had come to China prepared to accept martyrdom. She must be willing to accept the less dramatic martyrdom of loneliness and misunderstanding.

One of the younger O'Sullivan sisters was thinking at this time of following the footsteps of Molly and Enda and becoming a missionary nun. Molly wrote to give her advice and encourage-

69

ment. It is a revealing letter. It shows that in spite of her troubles she was as convinced as ever of the value of her vocation.

You said in your letter you had not my courage. It only requires a good square look at life and death. Death is the end of the road — and what comes after? How happy we will be to die when we can say to Our Lord, 'Here I am. I gave up everything for you in time, to be with you for ever in eternity.' Life's very short when I look back and I'm certain more than half my life is gone. What have I done? Nothing in comparison to what Our Lord has done for me.

If you feel you would like to be a nun, try it. It is not easy at first, but one becomes used to giving up things. You can see Enda and I are happy working away for Our Lord. Some days are easy and some are tough enough, but we have to suffer a little. Look at those in the world, what they suffer running after a happiness they can't catch. And even if they do hold on to it for a while, it fades and passes away like all things of this world. You would make a fine missionary, so think about it.

Enda wants a husband for you. I don't. I think you would be wasted. There is so much to be done for Our Lord in the world and very few to do it. This letter seems to be a speech but I don't like letting the best in life pass you by if a look at it from my point of view would help you to decide whether you're going to take the high road or the low, or just drift on in the misty flats, where the rest drift to and fro. A nun does not drift. She knows what she's doing and where she is going.

The sister followed her advice and entered the convent for a time but afterwards left and married and raised a family. Molly was rather disappointed at first. She herself knew what she was doing and where she was going and was always a little surprised when others failed to share her clear and simple view of life.

* * *

Christmas and Easter passed and summer came to Peking, the summer of 1939. In Europe tension was rising as the likelihood of war increased. In Peking life went on much as usual.

Away from the moderating influence of the sea, the city had a climate that veered from one extreme to the other. The bitter cold of winter gave way to sweltering heat in summer. Molly found the heat more trying than the cold and the habit she wore did not help. 'We have a turkish bath here every day — free, gratis and for nothing! Our "chins" have to be changed three times a day, so you can imagine the heat!'

A few outings varied the monotony of school life. On the Feast of Corpus Christi, Molly went out to the nearby parish church for the Blessed Sacrament procession. 'It puts heart into you when you hear and see all the Chinese praying.' The following week, on the Feast of the Sacred Heart, the convent's name-day, they had a picnic. The nuns and pupils taking part were brought to the picnic site in a procession of rickshaws. 'The joys of life in China when you go for a ride! It's like this:' — and in a corner of the letter Molly squeezed in a drawing of a coolie pulling a rickshaw with a nun lolling back luxuriously in the seat.

On 27 August, five days before the German invasion of Poland, Molly wrote to say the nuns had been reciting rosaries all that day to avert the danger of war in Europe. She was naturally worried about her family. Even though Ireland was expected to be neutral, there was no guarantee that this neutrality would be respected. At the very least, there were likely to be difficulties in sending and receiving letters. 'During the Great War, the nuns who were here did not hear from their people for nearly five years!'

She had other more immediate problems to worry about. Earlier that month the Yellow River burst its banks and caused severe flooding in Tientsin. The convent there was flooded up to the ceilings of the ground floor rooms. The nuns and girls were able to take refuge in the upper storey. Some of their neighbours were not so fortunate.

> It was pitiable to see the women floundering in the flood and the babies being snatched from their arms. The Chinese houses are only one storey high and the poor people are up on the roofs. They had nothing to eat for a week, some of them. The water burst the hatches and the city was under water in half an hour. Our nuns who came said anything like the filth and smell of the water they never saw. All kinds of animals have been drowned, cows, everything. Whole villages have been swept away.

The convent in Peking was filled with refugees from the flooded areas. Molly's classroom was turned into a children's dormitory. She herself was hard at work preparing meals for the visitors and enjoying every minute of it. She was always at home in the kitchen. 'I feel like a fish that has found its water. All Chinese nuns there. They speak a kind of French. The job of a lifetime to understand them.'

September saw the refugees leaving and the pupils returning for the new school year. Molly resumed her teaching with a new confidence and contentment. 'I'm back in the classes again and I like it very much now. I'm getting a little experience and it does teach.' Around this time she had a dream which shed some light on her frame of mind.

> I was dreaming of Father Dan the other night. I dreamt of the most extraordinary people, Willie O'Grady and several of that band. We were all at a dance, if you please, and I wanted to get home early and we couldn't start the car. The bell woke me and for a minute I did not realise where I was. I jumped for joy when I realised where I was. It was a very vivid dream. All the old crowd were in it. Talk about distractions that day!

There is something touching about the way that her thoughts, released in sleep from the vigilance of her waking self, went back to the happy days at Little Island and the dances in the big farmhouse kitchen at Moord. Then when she awoke and realised where she was, she jumped for joy. Somehow the phrase carries total conviction. She had made the choice, counted the cost, paid the price. And she was happy.

* * *

The European war had little effect at first on the convent in Peking. Letters continued to arrive from Ireland but at lengthening intervals. 'This week I received Norrie's very welcome letter. I cried when I got it as it was four months since I had a word of news.' Then gradually the letters ceased altogether. Her sister Nance writes:

> You will understand how grievous to her spirit and to ours was this cutting off from home. She thought we no longer bothered to write, which was anguishing for us. During

World War II a whole year's letters were returned to me from the GPO in Dublin, with an apology saying they had retained them and other mail for China, hoping to get them through somehow but failed. Eventually we got a hint from somewhere that 'Via Siberia' on the address gave a better chance of arrival — and some got through. Homesickness was always with her.

Only one letter from Molly got through in 1940. For some reason there was a temporary improvement in 1941 and her family received eight letters from her before the end of that year. It also meant that mail from Europe was being received in Peking. This was of particular concern to Molly as she was due to make her final profession in March 1941 but could not do so unless the necessary authorisation arrived from Rome. She was kept in suspense almost until the last moment. On 23 March she wrote:

I am in haste to send you the good news. At last I'm the spouse of Our Blessed Lord for ever. I made my vows on the 19th. It was certainly the happiest day I ever spent.

I think I told you in my letters I was not sure. Enda knew she was going to make hers some two months beforehand. But I knew the night before going on retreat, that was just a week before. And was I happy! I've been wondering what it will be like to go to heaven when one can be so happy on earth. It was a joy without alloy. And since then I'm walking on air, as we used say at home.

I expect you would like some details. I was on retreat for a week beforehand — of course, no class, but I spent the time I was not praying in the kitchen. Mother, you always said I was fond of the range. There it was easy to pray. It's a Chinese sister who is the cook and she is very nice.

After that, the day before the ceremony I was shaking all over. I was very excited. The next day I was as cool as an oyster. I was the only one for the ceremony. The altar was beautifully decorated; lilies and white roses. All the flowers were white except one little red rose. In the sanctuary a big blue carpet which covered the whole floor. You should see it to appreciate it.

The bishop of Peking performed the ceremony. Before,

he gave a fairly long sermon in which he spoke of the recompense we have for leaving all things and following Our Divine Lord; a hundredfold in this life and eternal life for those who take up their cross and follow the Master.

Two months later she was still walking on air. 'I'm feeling like a three-year-old since I made my final vows.' There was a lull in the war between Japan and China, which meant that life in Peking was almost normal. Petrol was scarce, which did not directly affect the nuns as they had no car. Bread and rice were available but only in small quantities and at inflated prices. But she was at pains to assure the family that she was not wasting away from starvation. 'If you saw me now, I resemble the bus in Thurles, as fat as a fool!'

During the summer holidays she buckled down seriously to her Japanese lessons. Every day there was an hour-long class in the language. With Japanese and Chinese and French spoken all around her, she longed to hear the sound of English again. 'I would like to hear an English sermon now. It is five years since I heard one. We have one every week in French. Don't worry, I understand. When we were small we used be told: Think in Irish. Now, if you please, I think in French.'

Her last letter of 1941 was written in September. She had resumed her classes and in addition was taking a number of pupils for private piano lessons. She was well, though still overweight. 'I am a regular Mary Roundy now. I got fat since last year.' It was the last her family were to hear from her for four years.

* * *

Early on the morning of 7 December 1941 the Japanese air force attacked the American naval base at Pearl Harbour in the Hawaiian Islands. Japan was now at war with the United States and the British Commonwealth. Within the space of three months, most of south-east Asia was overrun by Japanese armies. Thailand, Malaya, Hong Kong, Singapore, Burma, the Philippines, the Dutch East Indies were all taken before the Allies could rally their forces. The Empire of the Rising Sun seemed as invincible in the East as the Third Reich was in the West.

The position of Europeans in the Japanese-occupied territories changed overnight. Those who were citizens of the US or the British Commonwealth automatically became enemy aliens and were liable to imprisonment. French citizens were exempt since France had surrendered to Hitler, but French Canadians were not. The Japanese began rounding up Europeans, including missionaries, and interning them in concentration camps. Conditions in the camps varied. Captured soldiers were treated with great brutality because any soldier who did not fight to the death was regarded as a coward who had forfeited all right to life. Civilians were somewhat better treated but hunger and disease killed many, even in the civilian camps.

The nuns in the Sacred Heart Convent were left alone for more than a year. A small group of ageing women who rarely left the house in which they lived were obviously no threat to the security of the state. However, things changed in early 1943 as the American and British counter-attack began to recapture lost ground.

One day in March a Japanese officer arrived at the convent and produced a list of nuns who were classified as enemy aliens. They were to pack their belongings and be ready to leave for the concentration camp on the following Monday. The five nuns on his list included Mother Eamonn O'Sullivan, who was described as a British citizen. 'I'm Irish', said Molly indignantly. 'It's the same thing', said the officer.

Molly was so furious she forgot to be frightened. She rounded on the officer and in a combination of fractured Japanese, French and English told him that a British subject was the last thing she would ever allow anyone to call her. In fact, she and her country had recently fought a long and bitter war to ensure that they were not and never would be subject to British rule. The officer, whose knowledge of the Irish war of independence was understandably sketchy, was taken aback by her onslaught. He was even more taken aback when her sense of humour suddenly got the better of her and she began to laugh, tickled at the absurdity of being threatened with imprisonment for being British. He began to laugh too, perhaps out of politeness or perhaps to humour this mad European woman, and promised to make inquiries at headquarters regarding the status of Irish citizens.

The following Monday the lorries arrived to collect the prisoners. There were now only four names on the list. Molly was free to stay in the convent.

The other four were taken to a concentration camp at Wiesien, a short distance south of Tientsin. There they found a large number of missionaries, including nuns from many different orders. The Franciscan Missionaries of Mary alone totalled twenty-eight. The FMMs were all housed in the same block and they managed to establish a kind of community life for themselves. They were not physically ill-treated and their greatest hardship was the food, which was both bad and scarce. They dreaded the coming of winter.

Happily for them, it occurred to somebody high up that it would be a good idea to put the nuns under house arrest in one of their own convents. This would take the responsibility of housing and feeding them off the shoulders of the authorities. So in August 1943 the twenty-eight FMMs were all sent to the Sacred Heart Convent in Peking, regardless of where they had come from originally. They were forbidden to leave the convent, which was no great hardship, or to teach, which was. But it was a great relief to be back in one of their own houses after five months in the camp.

The community in Peking now numbered about fifty, twice its normal size. Molly, who always enjoyed company, found this congenial. Moreover, the increase in the community meant that there were more singers available for the nuns' choir on ceremonial occasions. She would look back on the period from 1943 to 1945 as a golden age for church music in the Sacred Heart Convent.

There was one aspect of the situation that she found less pleasant. Up to this she had been teaching English to junior classes only. Now that the other English-speaking nuns were banned from teaching she had to take on the senior classes. She found this daunting as she felt she had no particular qualification for teaching English apart from the fact that it was her mother tongue. However it turned out to be easier than she had expected and she continued to teach senior English even after the war had ended.

The end came quite unexpectedly. On 6 August 1945 the Americans dropped the first atom bomb on Hiroshima. Three days later they dropped a second one on Nagasaki. On 14 August Japan surrendered. The Japanese in Peking laid down their arms as obediently as they had taken them up and north China returned to its familiar state of chaos.

8

LIBERATION

Another conquering army entered Peking. This time it was the Americans. Jeeps and lorries came roaring through the streets, filled with breezy young GIs. One of their first stops was at the Sacred Heart Convent, where they dumped a load of soap, condensed milk, tinned food and other provisions in front of the hall door. 'Sister, all you need now is a tin-opener!' they shouted as they zoomed off again. After years of bread and rice, the nuns could only weep at the abundance.

Many of the American soldiers had been educated by nuns themselves and they gladly took the Sacred Heart community under their wing. There was the young GI who saved up his ration of chocolate for them when he heard they had not seen a sweet since the beginning of the war. There was the street-wise Irish-American from Chicago who raided the Red Cross units to get them medical supplies. There was the New Yorker whose mother sent him twelve woolly vests for the winter which he passed on to the nuns. These and many others were long remembered in the convent with gratitude and affection.

The transport facilities of the US forces were ready to help priests and nuns who were trying to return to their missions. Most of the roads and railways had been destroyed during the war and there were large areas in the interior which could be reached only by air. Some of the missionaries carried by the American Air Force had been waiting six or seven years for an opportunity of getting to their allotted missions.

The greatest joy of all was the re-opening of communications with home. Molly's first letter to her mother in four years was written on 26 August. It was packed full with questions about everything that had been happening to the family during what she called 'the dark ages'.

> Make Kate write to me giving me all the news. It is not because I'm buried in the back of beyond that I'm not interested in all and every one of your doings. Blood is thicker than water and I think when one becomes a religious and gives oneself to God that we love our own more than ever. My prayers are morning, noon and night for all of you.
>
> What about Dad's grave? Is everything fixed up and very nice? He is ten years dead RIP. How time flies! And Uncle Pat — I cannot pray for one without the other. Send a photo of grave please. What about Barr's exam? Is he qualified? And Norrie? Where? What? And how? And Pam? Has she 'a notion of taking the vows'? Nancy and Enda are doing God's work if they are not sick, and even then they can save souls. Eamonn, I pray a lot for you because you have the hard job of keeping the home fires burning. . . .
>
> God love, bless and keep you always.

The situation in Peking was still unstable. The threat of a communist take-over had not receded. Large areas of China were under communist control and Russian armies were massed on the border not far away. Molly believed that the presence of US forces in Peking was caused by fear of the victorious Russians rather than the defeated Japanese.

For the Japanese, she still had sympathy and respect and she contrasted them favourably with the Chinese. 'The Chinese have no sense of nationality or honour. For a Chinese it is a crime to belong to the army, it being the lowest position in society. The Japs were quite the contrary. They have a deep sense of nationality and took their beating very well. But in the Philippines they did some terrible things.' One of the victims in the Philippines was her own first cousin, John O'Sullivan, a layman who had been working with the missionaries and who showed great resourcefulness in obtaining food and clothing and other supplies for war refugees. He and two Irish priests were arrested one day by the Japanese and never seen again. Molly found it difficult to reconcile stories of this kind with what she had seen of Japanese behaviour in Peking.

There was to follow for her and for the Christians of China

a short period of peace and progress. The three years 1946, 1947 and 1948 were years during which the Church was able to live its life and do its work in freedom. In all the twenty-eight years Molly spent in Peking, this was the only time that approached normality. These three years, sandwiched between the tensions of the Japanese occupation and the dark night of communism, were an opportunity for growth and upbuilding that was used to the full.

A sign of the times was the announcement early in 1946 that Pius XII had decided to nominate Peking's Archbishop Thomas Tien to the College of Cardinals, the first native of China ever to receive this honour. Molly was delighted to hear the news and her delight was widely shared. 'The Chinese are so proud of him. Even the pagans say ''our Cardinal''. They have no notion of what it means but it does not matter. They have someone of their own high up in the Church of Rome.'

The newly created Cardinal returned to his native land on 29 June 1946, the Feast of Saints Peter and Paul. It was an occasion of widespread celebration, especially for the Catholics of Peking. Molly sent home a description of the day's events.

Last Saturday our new Chinese Cardinal, who is also Archbishop of Peking, arrived here by aeroplane. There was great excitement about it. All the Catholic bodies (which are not like the Catholic bodies at home: here we live in a very pagan city) were brought together to welcome him.

It reminded me of the Eucharistic Congress — every type of vehicle, lorries packed with priests, nuns, children, boy scouts, university students, who of course did most of the shouting. We had to go to an airfield outside the city. We saw the plane coming down and we were not there yet — it was a race. When the long stream of cars arrived, we had to get out, lift our skirts and run to be in time. It was funny to see some of the very dignified congregation running.

Finally, we got there first and our Rev. Mother Provincial was nearly the first to kiss his ring. Then it was time to come back to the Cathedral. We walked sedately back to our cars and followed in procession. Then there was the ceremony in the church. He arrived in all his robes of office.

All I could pray for was that he would not faint with the heat. Then he made his entrance, preceded by the choir and all the clergy. The Pope's Bull was read in Latin, French, English and Chinese. God help me — eight years in China and I cannot speak a word of Chinese!

An even more joyful occasion for the nuns of the Sacred Heart Convent came later that same year. On 24 November the Pope beatified the so-called Shansi martyrs, those who had died at Taiyuanfu in Shansi province during the Boxer Rising of 1900. They included seven Franciscan Missionaries of Mary, the first members of the order to receive the honour of beatification.

The community in the Sacred Heart Convent included a survivor of the massacre, Sister Mary Frances. She was not killed with the others, either because of her youth or because she was the only Chinese among the sisters. She had been forced to watch the others die and then drink their blood. To refuse would have meant that she was disowning her sisters and the cause for which they died.

I suppose Enda told you that our seven martyred sisters are going to be beatified on the 24th of November. They were killed in this province, a day and a half's journey from Peking. Some of our sisters have gone to Rome. One, who is seventy, was tortured when the others were killed and she was made drink a bowl of hot blood taken from those who had been killed. It would have amounted to apostasy if she had not done so. Another one, her father, was left as dead. They gave him a fierce blow of the axe but his pigtail saved him. The blow glanced off the hair. He was badly injured all the same. I'm sure the Pope will be pleased to see these relics of 1900.

Last month one woman died at eighty-six. She saw her husband cut up before her. She had five children. In China the boys and girls are dressed alike so you cannot tell which is which. The soldiers asked her which were the boys. She pointed them out. They killed them. She had one little baby at her breast. They asked her, was it a boy or a girl. She replied, 'It's a boy'. They took it and killed it. He was fifteen months. They then violated the eldest girl and left. She was the mother of three martyrs and the wife of one. The four are being beatified. She was a brave woman. I think she should be canonised herself.

80

With the letter she enclosed holy pictures of the seven martyred nuns for all the family. In all her years in the convent, this was the only real present she was ever able to give them. Even the cards she sent them at Christmas were second-hand, put together with scissors and paste from the cards she herself had received the previous Christmas. It was one of the ways in which she lived her vow of poverty.

*　*　*

As long as the American troops remained in China, the situation would remain stable. Once they were withdrawn, civil war seemed inevitable. The nationalist government of Chiang Kai Shek was weak and riddled with corruption. The communists under the leadership of Mao Tse Tung were strong and ruthless and backed by Russia. It required no great gifts of prophecy to forecast that there was every likelihood of China being under communist control by 1950.

The communists were active on the political as well as the military front. They had secret supporters and fellow-travellers throughout the country, in government, in universities and schools, in the media. They were pushing the message that Chinese communism was different, that it sought only to rectify social injustice, and that it had no quarrel with religion. The reality of life in areas ruled by communists showed how false this picture was.

The Christians had little illusion about what would happen to them under communism. It would be the Boxer Rising all over again, except that this time there would be no European armies to come to the rescue. Molly's letters at this time often refer to the persecution of Christians in the Red areas. The same letter that describes the death of the Shansi martyrs contains information about the current situation from refugees who were staying in the convent.

> News from here is pretty much the same. Fighting all over the place. At the moment we have ten Franciscan sisters (not our own), refugees from the dearg region. They went through some awful things. They and twenty-two priests were locked up in the same room for several days. They were allowed out twice a day. They had two cups of millet (bird seed) gruel per day. This is a grain which gives us

Europeans summer cholera, so you can imagine the result. They are happy to be here. They have lost everything, convent, dispensary, orphanage, native sisters, all. After more than twenty years their work is reduced to nothing.

God's ways are not our ways. These have suffered because they are Christians. I hope the dearg have no hold in Ireland. You should see and hear, to know what brutes men can become under its sway.

It is interesting to notice Molly's use of the word *dearg* (the Irish word for 'red') to denote communists. It was her first venture into a system of code-words that was to become more elaborate as time went on. She suspected with good reason that mail was being tampered with by communist sympathisers in the postal service.

The only thing the Christians could do was to work while the light lasted. They were preparing a Church for the catacombs. Every effort was made to build up the community of believers in readiness for the dark times to come. For Molly and the nuns of the Sacred Heart Convent, this meant doing their daily work as well as they could, giving a sound religious education to the girls in their care and strengthening their faith to withstand the trials that lay ahead.

After the difficulties of the war years, the convent school was back to normal and, indeed, flourishing. There were now around 1,000 pupils on the rolls, 300 in the European school and 700 in the Chinese. The European school, which had been the worst affected, was profiting by the big influx of diplomats, businessmen and military personnel from the western countries. One of Molly's new pupils in 1946 was a fifteen-year-old American girl called Breen O'Brien. Twenty years later, after Molly's death, she remembered her as 'a happy, pudgy 39-year-old nun who delighted in surprises. Her large, soft shoes padded noiselessly along the loose square tiles in the hallways and we were often dismayed by her sudden appearance at the doorway when we were busy with autograph books instead of the précis she had left us to copy.'

Molly taught Breen a wide range of subjects, including piano and biology. Her teacher's desk doubled as a laboratory and she would sit there placidly dissecting a bird or a fish and ignoring the girls' squeals of protest when she asked them to identify the dismembered parts.

I will always remember that classroom on a sunny corner of the second floor of the large brick school building. The very high latticed windows even had curtains on them, a nicety not often found in high schools. A moulding ran along the top of the windows, and pipes from the radiator ran up the inner corner of the room to the left of Mother's desk as I sat facing her. I believe the radiators themselves were something of a formality, as they barely provided an hour's warmth during the bitter cold winter months. I don't know what Mother wore under her ivory serge habit to keep her warm; she did always have a small woolly shawl around her shoulders. But I know that I have never piled one layer upon another more than I did to sit comfortably in our classroom. Most of us kept on our leather fur-lined boots over a few pairs of wool stockings, in addition to our slacks or leggings decorously covered by our blue cotton uniform dresses and sweaters. We wore an enamelled school pin in the centre of our white Peter Pan collars; the inscription said *Ad caritatem per veritatem*. To complete the decor of the room, lovely framed prints hung on the wall, artistically arranged; before one of the windows was a feathery fern plant on its own stand.

Breen O'Brien's most enduring memories of Molly centred on the convent chapel where Molly both sang and played the organ. 'I shall never forget midnight Mass on Christmas Eve in that little holy room. The angelic nuns in their white serge habits and veils as they floated up to the choir loft, and the altar ablaze with myriad candles and Christmas plants — all seemed to me like a foretaste of the sweetness of heaven. Mother Eamonn's beautifully developed voice did much to enhance this effect.'

* * *

In those years after the war, Peking became, in Molly's words, 'a little Rome'. It was the centre of Catholic life and organisation for the whole of the country. Most of the religious orders working in China opened houses in Peking. Among them were the Columban Fathers, whose members were almost all Irish. They set up a house where Columbans coming to China for the first time could study the language and customs of the country. Molly was delighted. It meant that she could see Irish faces and hear Irish voices and get the latest news from Ireland.

Some of the Columbans who came to see her in the convent brought presents from home, a shawl from Mother Patern and a box of rosary beads from Nance. Another brought news of Enda (Mother Fergus), who had returned from Liberia and was now novice mistress in Loughglynn. He was met in the convent parlour by Molly, accompanied as usual by another nun.

> He looked at her and said, 'You are Mother Fergus's sister'. She looked at me. I said, 'No, she is not. I am Mother's sister'. He was in doubt. I think he thought I was codding him. So he asked me three times. Finally I laughed. Then he believed me. He said the laugh was the same. But he could not conceive how anybody as small and fat as me could be your ladyship's sister. I was weighed the other day. Don't tell anybody but I turned the scales at 12st 7lb.

The most memorable of these Columban visitors was a Dublin priest, Father Aedan McGrath, who arrived unexpectedly at the convent on 20 August 1948. 'Sister Eamonn opened the door of their convent in Peking when I went in the hope of starting the Legion in your lovely school', he wrote later. 'She jumped in the hall when she heard where I was from and shouted "Up de Valera!" '

He told her his story in the convent parlour. He had been appointed by Mgr Riberi, the Papal Nuncio, to set up cells or praesidia of the Legion of Mary throughout China. The Legion of Mary had been founded in Dublin in 1921 by Frank Duff as an organisation for lay Catholics who wished to engage in charitable and apostolic work. It had spread rapidly throughout Ireland and then been carried by Irish missionaries to many parts of the world. He himself had started the Legion in his own mission in Central China and found it a most effective way of forming lay apostles and training them in leadership. Would Molly like to help him to start the Legion in Peking?

Molly knew little about the Legion of Mary but she was willing to try. She immediately set about the task of starting a praesidium among her pupils. On 3 September she wrote to tell her mother about the Legion.

> I remember it before I entered, but it was very young and I remember Dan Dawson giving out about it. But now it

has spread all over the world and the bishops here are very anxious that the religion would be spread by this means. Can you imagine that we are three million Catholics in China with five hundred million pagans? It would take some personnel to supply the wants, so the Nuncio wants to try out the Legion. I believe he was Mgr Robinson's secretary in Ireland for some years, so he knows all about it. Say a few prayers it will be a success and that many souls will be saved by its means. We had our first meeting here today and began with six. I was hoping for larger numbers but I suppose Our Lady knows what she wants, so that's that.

Her letters for the rest of 1948 chart the progress of the Legion in the school and in the city. In October she reported that the Chinese version of the Legion of Mary handbook was being printed. 'It is costing a small fortune and Father is stony broke, but he has made Our Lady the banker as it is her work. She has got to find the money.' By December sixteen of the twenty-five Catholic girls in the European school were members of Molly's praesidium.

Most of the Legionaries belong to pagan families and have the job of trying to convert their mothers and fathers and brothers and sisters. Some priests have come in contact with the families and are working away to break down the wrong ideas that might have been in these heads. You know, these girls would make you feel ashamed. They are willing to face all kinds of hard work for Our Lord. When they are insulted, they feel that they have done something for him.

I believe the Legion is doing fine work in Peking. In one parish in which the Jesuits are in charge they have seven praesidia. That is wonderful in a pagan city. Our Lady was crowned Queen of China about four years ago and seems to be taking her job seriously at last.

* * *

The setting up of the Legion of Mary was part of the process of preparing the Church for life under communism. It was expected that the communists would expel or imprison all priests and nuns and that the future of the Church in China would depend largely on the laity. The rapid spread of the Legion in

Peking and throughout the country was one sign of hope for the future.

Despite the uncertain situation, there were many conversions during this period. Molly's letters describe numerous instances, some of them hearsay, others among her own pupils. Her own faith was very simple and even childlike and this comes out in her descriptions.

> Did I ever tell you about my fight with the Little Flower? Well, last year I had a girl ready to be baptised. Her parents would not give consent, so she was hesitating. One day I suddenly decided she should be baptised on the 15th of August. On the 12th she came to me and said she could not.
>
> St Thérèse was in her place of state on my desk. I said nothing to the girl but I looked at the Little Flower and said, 'We have to do our own duty. I'd like to know what you're doing in heaven, anyway. You're not keeping your promise'. So I took the picture and said, 'Now, you're going into punishment in my drawer and you will not come out until she is baptised'. Would you believe it, the child was baptised within twenty-four hours after that scene.
>
> You know, I believe with the saints, if you treat them like your own on earth, a scolding now and again does no harm. So St Thérèse is still on my desk but now I need only threaten her, and believe me she does not like going into my drawer.

When it came to conversions, she was not interested in numbers only. She wanted her converts to have a real relationship with God. The following year she wrote:

> We had two baptisms here on the 15th of August. It is always on that day that I have a few. I asked one the other day her idea of God. She said, 'God is like the atmosphere. He is everywhere and sees everything. God is an intelligent atmosphere, as it were'. Sometimes they give answers that astonish one. It shows that they think of these things when alone.
>
> I asked, 'Does that bring you nearer God?' 'Well', she said, 'we cannot live without air, our bodies die. In the same way we cannot live without God, our souls die. We cannot do without air or escape from it, neither can we do

without God or escape from him.' I think that this one realises what the presence of God is.

The American troops were withdrawn in March 1947, but it was not until the latter part of 1948 that the communist forces began their decisive advance. In the meantime they had been softening up the opposition in various ways: firstly, by convincing them that resistance to the advance of communism was doomed to failure, and secondly, by promising them that all their freedoms would be preserved, including freedom of religion. As part of this strategy, they allowed some foreign missionaries back into the areas under their control.

The missionary orders were not impressed by these assurances. They found themselves in a dilemma when the Red army began to threaten Peking in October 1948. Should they go or should they stay? The arguments in favour of going were obvious: the difficulty of operating under Red rule, the likelihood that they would be expelled anyhow, the many other mission-fields where they were equally needed and would have far more freedom of action. But there were also reasons for staying. It was hard to have to leave the churches they had built, the hospitals and schools they had worked in, the people they had come to know and love. Should they not stay with them in their hour of trial and share their sufferings if necessary? And was it not possible that some way of living under communism might eventually be worked out?

At the beginning of November foreigners began to leave Peking on the advice of their embassies. Among them were many missionaries, especially those who were studying there and those who had been driven from their missions in the interior. The nuns in the Sacred Heart Convent wished to stay and sent word to their Mother General in Rome. They did not want to leave their Chinese sisters, their school children, the poor people they tended in their dispensary. They wanted to have at least one place in the city where the Blessed Sacrament would be exposed and honoured and intercession made each day.

The Mother General directed that each foreign-born nun could make her own decision whether to stay or go. All the nuns chose to stay. Writing home with the news, Molly described the night in Rome ten years earlier when she and her companions had been given a similar choice.

Mother General told us now was the time to stay at home if we were afraid to go and replace our sisters who were killed. Not one of us budged. I said to myself, 'You will have to pass out sometime and you might as well do it fighting for a good cause.' I never regretted keeping my mouth shut that night. Even though we've had some tough parts to jump over, we always got the grace we needed for the day'.

Soon afterwards the Mother General sent a second directive, countermanding the first. It said that all non-Chinese nuns under forty were to leave China. Those over forty were to have the option of staying. Molly was forty-one. She stayed. On 27 December she wrote home:

I was allowed remain in Peking and I could not tell you what a consolation that was to me. I felt Our Lord was not very displeased with me because he left me here. Sink or swim, so to speak anyway, I felt that he thought I would come up to scratch in an emergency. I feel as if I won't be kept out of heaven. Talk about being happy! I feel as if I were walking on air.

9

THE PEOPLE'S REPUBLIC

By the end of December the Red army had encircled the city of Peking. They delayed their entry into the city for two reasons. One was to soften up the civilian population by letting them experience the hardships of a winter siege, with its hunger and cold and breakdowns in public services. The other was to enter into secret negotiations with the military commander of Peking. He agreed to surrender the city after no more than a token resistance and as a reward was given the post of Minister of Water Conservancy when the new communist government was formed.

On 1 February 1949, the Red army entered Peking. Those who expected an orgy of looting and rioting were to be disappointed. The entry of the People's Liberation Army into the ancient capital of China was carefully planned and stage-managed. A disciplined army in spotless uniforms and infection masks, with bayonets and buttons gleaming, marched eight abreast through the streets. All day long the nuns in the Sacred Heart Convent could hear the steady tramp of marching feet, the pounding rhythm that signalled the end of the old order and the beginning of the new. The corruption and confusion of the past was over. The new era of peace, prosperity and progress had dawned.

The fall of Peking was to prove decisive. Whatever fighting spirit was left in the nationalist forces deserted them. The Red army swept down the coast, capturing Shanghai in May and Canton in October. Chiang Kai-Shek and the remnants of his forces withdrew to Taiwan. By the end of 1949 Mao Tse-tung was master of all the Chinese mainland. The country was re-named the People's Republic of China with Peking as its capital.

The Constitution of the People's Republic guaranteed freedom of religion. All citizens had the right to believe and to worship according to their faith. They could not be discriminated against or punished because of their religious beliefs. But the government of the People's Republic, like every other government, had the right and the duty to punish those who engaged in activities contrary to the good of the people.

The worthlessness of the constitutional guarantees soon became apparent. The Christians of China found themselves the object of an organised and ruthless persecution. Bishops and priests were arrested in their thousands, layfolk in their tens of thousands. Their trials, when they were allowed have trials, bore no resemblance to normal administration of justice. The real reason for their arrest, their religion, was never mentioned. Instead, they were accused of a variety of fantastic crimes against the People's Republic.

The evidence produced in court was of the flimsiest kind. A letter written to someone in the United States proved that the writer was working for the CIA. A report sent to a superior in Rome was evidence that the sender had been gathering information and engaging in espionage. The mildest complaint about shortages of food and other commodities was part of a plot to stir up unrest and overthrow the government. Witnesses were forced to make false accusations under the threat of being imprisoned themselves if they refused. As a last resort, if all else failed, the accused person could be made to confess to a long litany of crimes through a combination of brainwashing, starvation, torture and drugs. Those found guilty were sentenced to long terms of imprisonment in jails or labour camps. No-one was ever acquitted. The people's justice never failed.

The persecution weighed most heavily on the Chinese Christians. Most of the missionaries, priests and nuns, were simply served with deportation orders and expelled from the country. Other missionaries were put on trial and sentenced to prison but were usually released and deported before their sentence was finished. There was no compassion in this: the government wished to avoid the embarrassment of having missionaries dying in prison.

Deportation was not an option for the Chinese Christians. The sentences they were given had to be served to the last minute of the last day. The only chance of an earlier release was through death, and many of them did die in prison as result of their sufferings.

All this lay in the future on that cold day in February as the People's Liberation Army took possession of Peking and the red flag was hoisted over the old palace of the emperors. The nuns of the Sacred Heart Convent had made their decision to stay. Now they had to live with it.

* * *

The remainder of Molly's life, seventeen and a half years, was spent under the red flag. During all that period she continued to write home at an average rate of once a month and her letters arrived regularly and punctually. But they were different from the letters she had been writing before, shorter, more cryptic, needing to be interpreted.

These letters were written under a triple censorship. The first and most obvious was the official government censorship which read every letter with the most careful attention and was constantly watching for anything that could be considered in any way offensive to the government. Occasionally, Molly managed to bypass the censor but she still had to be careful of what she said, in case the letter fell into the wrong hands.

The second censorship was that of her own superiors. The rule was that letters had to be handed unsealed to the Reverend Mother for posting. In many convents this rule was only a formality but not in Peking. In 1948 a new superior, Mother Mary Olga Sofia, had been appointed and Molly found her easier to get on with than her predecessor. The Mother Provincial, Mother Mary of the Cross, also lived in the Peking convent during the communist years. She had overall responsibility for all the FMM convents in north China, though by the end of her time there the only one still functioning normally was the Sacred Heart Convent. Many of Molly's letters to her mother have little greetings added in the vacant space at the top and signed M.S. or M.C. These greetings for Mrs O'Sullivan were well meant but they indicate that the letters were read by one or other of the superiors. No matter how good Molly's relations were with them, it must have had an inhibiting effect on what she wrote.

The third censorship was that imposed by those she wrote to, particularly her mother. As the years passed and the persecution mounted, newspapers told harrowing stories of missionaries expelled from China, photographs showed their emaciated faces, books described their ordeals. Molly's family were in permanent fear for her safety and for her life. She tried to make light of the danger and to play down the suffering. Only very rarely did she let the mask slip and reveal the constant tension and pressure that was the background to her daily life during all these years.

Shortly before the fall of Peking she had written to her sister Enda suggesting an elementary code that might escape the censor's notice.

> If we can write we will let you know what it is like. If I write in red ink, you will know it is very bad. If in blue, life is more or less normal. If in red, you can take the opposite of everything I say because we will have to praise the bridge whether it is good or bad.

As a code, it was obviously not very well thought out. It is not always easy to know what the opposite of a statement may be. The opposite of 'The authorities are treating us well' would presumably be 'The authorities are not treating us well'. But what would be the opposite of a statement like 'Our Blessed Sacrament procession last week was well attended'? Would it mean that our procession last week was badly attended? Or not attended at all? Or did not take place? Or did take place but not last week?

Molly's first letter to her mother after the fall of Peking was typed, not handwritten, and in it she said: 'Tell Enda I would write to her in red ink as requested but I have no red typing ribbon at the moment. Tell her everything is A.1.' This may be an attempt to tell Enda that things were far from A.1 without alarming her mother, but it is not very clear. At any rate, she soon forgot about the red ink code and relied instead on the use of Irish words and references which would be understood by her family but not by the censor. Her sister Nance became an expert at decoding these references.

> The garden and plants referred to the community. The yellow roses were the native sisters, Paschal was the Bishop, and Dan or Sagart were the priests. Mère was the Mother General. The prisons were all named after a jail in England

or Ireland, and so on. Gone on holiday usually meant gone to jail.

The use of Irish words was Molly's most frequent ploy. Her knowledge of Irish had become rusty over the years and her spelling was not always what it should be, but she usually managed to make her meaning clear. *Dia* was God, *Iosagán* was Jesus, *Muire* was Mary. *Máire* referred to Molly herself. *Eaglais* meant church and *aifreann* (variously spelt) meant Mass. She had evidently forgotten the Irish words for Confession and Communion. She uses the words *arán beatha*, which literally mean bread of life, to denote Communion. For Confession, she speaks about spring-cleaning or scraping the skillet or some such phrase.

Mother Thomas à Becket from Scotland was with Molly all during these years in Peking. Before her death she visited Nance and gave her much valuable information about the period. This helped to clarify many of Molly's coded references. But there are still passages which are hard to understand. The fact is that Molly's nature was too open and simple for any kind of organised deviousness. She would have made a bad spy.

For the first few weeks after the fall of Peking, the nuns were allowed to continue their normal routine of work and prayer. Molly's first letter under the new regime made no more than passing references to food shortages and other difficulties:

> I received a letter from you during the week and it was a real surprise. I was so glad to hear that everyone and everything is on the baker's list. So am I, *Deo Gratias*. The news is scarce over here (and the praties also!) . . . We must take our medicine — and no grinning. I have quite a lot to take nowadays but I feel the cure will be complete. I will be self-forgetful by the time the dose is complete.

Then one day in June the interrogators arrived. One by one, the nuns were questioned about their past histories in the minutest detail while copious notes were taken. None of the nuns knew the purpose of the questions, what hidden traps they might be falling into, what fate lay in store for them. They knew that wholesale executions of political opponents were taking place throughout the country. The strain was intense. Molly wrote:

> All our places are still going full steam ahead. We have a dispensary here now and souls are being sent heavenward

very often. Our sisters left one house in Harbin but are living in a small one beside it. The Rev. Mother writes and says it is a great grace to live nowadays because we have to live our vocation to the full.

It is most amusing to see how curious some people are. It does not do to say, 'Questions that should not be asked need not be answered.'

Goodbye now, may God love and bless every one of you till you hear from me again. When? That is in the hands of the Almighty. He is playing his own will with us now.

The last sentence had been a favourite saying of her father whenever things were looking black.

The nuns were made to write out detailed accounts of their lives which were collected and taken away. They were then left in peace for a few weeks. But at the beginning of August the inquisitors had evidently returned, because Molly was writing to say the garden was full of microscopic animals called *dearg* that get 'under your skin to see what colour your blood is.'

> Yet these animals also have their uses. They work in communities and are very industrious. If we had half their energy, things would not be like they are. They are united also, which is a lot in their favour. I hope somebody finds a way of getting rid of them, because they are more annoying than mosquitoes. Between mosquitoes at night and dearg by day, ours is a nice 'ouse, ours is.

Some of the interrogation sessions lasted for five or six hours at a time in the heat of a Peking summer. After a particularly gruelling session, Molly would often head for the piano and relieve her feelings in a burst of Beethoven or some soothing Brahms. She never knew whether she had given the right or the wrong answers to the questions she was asked. Time alone would tell:

> Life is pretty much the same. We had a little exam in a Ballykinlar fashion. I think I passed mine . . . This year I will not have to meditate on hell. I have a fair idea of what it is like — perpetual torment, we are told — so there is nothing like getting a touch of it beforehand. It helps one to concentrate on spiritual matters and make a firm resolution to avoid that spot hereafter.

The censor could hardly be expected to know that Ballykinlar was an internment camp during the Irish war of independence.

* * *

The pattern of 1949 was continued and intensified in 1950 as the new government strengthened its grip upon the Chinese mainland. For the first time in most people's memories the country had a single central and effective government. Fighting was at an end. Law and order prevailed. The gap between rich and poor was narrowing. The currency was stable and food prices were controlled. Administration and public services were functioning. Bribery was a thing of the past. The trains ran on time.

These things were bought at a price. Human life and liberty were of little account. The rights of the individual were of no importance compared with the good of the people. The Triple Autonomy or Three-Self Movement was launched with the aim of making China self-sufficient and free from all foreign influence. The three selfs were self-support, self-government and self-propagation. Anything or anyone that stood in the way of the three selfs must be ruthlessly swept away.

One of the main obstacles to the three selfs was the Christian religion and in particular the Catholic Church. Catholics were officially considered to be more dangerous than Protestants because they owed allegiance to a foreign ruler, the Pope. The leaders of the Catholic community, clerical and lay, were singled out for attack. Every effort was made to have them accused by their fellow Catholics of being traitors to their country and conspirators against the government. Many leading Catholics were thrown into prison. Those who remained at liberty were subjected to a constant round of denunciations and interrogations.

The nuns in the Sacred Heart Convent were kept under pressure. Chinese parents were now afraid to send their children to be educated by foreigners and so there was a steady fall in the number of pupils in the Chinese school. The European school also suffered, as the number of foreigners living in Peking was far smaller than before. Apart from other considerations, this brought severe financial problems for the nuns, since their only income came from school fees.

On top of all this, the interrogators were liable to return to the convent at any time. During Lent Molly had to undergo the penance of a female interrogator who not only questioned her but ransacked her room for incriminating evidence. Molly was almost brought to breaking point, as her Easter letter shows.

It is a penance to write a letter. I have so much I must éist do bhéal [keep silent] about. I could write reams and possibly some day I will but at the moment I have no time and various other reasons.

The dearg that was sent is not at all nice. It has turned out like a fox or a wolverine. I think this last is nearer the mark. She tears everything to pieces, causes disorder all over the house. She seems to think everything she finds in my room belongs to her and was made for her to destroy. I thought she may be some good for rats or mice, but all vermin are friends of hers, I think. I hope something happens her soon for I haven't the heart to poison her. I would like to tar and feather her. Some of the old methods of Queen Bess — and these would be too mild.

Do you know quite a number of sagarts have been given a short cut across the Jordan [put to death]? They have gone home to do some interceding for the ones that are left in the lurch. This Lent was not like any other for me. I understood better the sufferings of the Master, and sure we are not above him. I'm nearly 15 years working for him and the longer you're at it the more you realise that there is nothing else worth doing. He is the only constant in a world of change.

These visitations continued on into the summer. In a letter dated Ascension Day she mentions the song *Spring in Donegal* and goes on:

You know maybe, or perhaps you do not, that we have a pest of bobbies, as we used to call them back at home. Yesterday we had an influx and I could not get rid of them. They behave like buzzing bees and after their exit I was more or less upset, to say the least of it. I boned a music mag. Says I to myself says I, 'There is only one way to raise your heart — that is, a touch of the old pianner'. So I sat down and enjoyed myself for half an hour. It was while

> I was there I fell on the above song. Did I enjoy myself!
> I could hear Father Dan sing it with his tenor. It is funny
> how a little bit of home affects one in this country. When
> I fall on something which spells of the old land, it takes
> me back to my own lovely Lee.

She had only one consoling piece of news. 'The Legion is doing its bit all right. It is in every parish now, I think.'

The summer holidays found her at her lowest ebb. Interrogations, searches, arrest of some friends, disappearance of others, the knowledge that the next knock at the door could be for her, all combined to fill her days and nights with tension. There were financial worries, food shortages, health problems. In July she had a very painful crop of boils which lasted until the end of the hot weather. Her sense of isolation was increased by the lack of letters from her brothers and sisters. In an uncharacteristically bitter outburst she wrote to her mother, 'They have no time to be bothered with their elder sister in China who, you know as well as I do, gave that crowd the best years of my life. But eaten bread is soon forgotten.'

She brightened up with the coming of autumn and the resumption of school. A highlight for her was the proclamation by Pius XII of the dogma of the Assumption of the Blessed Virgin Mary, which took place on 1 November 1950. Her life-long devotion to the Mother of God showed itself in the letter she wrote to her sister Enda a few days later.

> What kind of a feast did you have for the dogma of the
> Assumption? Here we had three Masses, one by a bishop.
> The chapel was beautifully decorated. Our Lady was placed
> on a high pedestal. Up over her head a canopy in the form
> of a crown of golden silk and down in front were six angels,
> three on each side, holding up silver cups (these latter made
> of paper), at the feet of each angel a bouquet of carnations.
> The whole thing looked like heaven.
>
> On the pillars, at least on five, there were crowns of roses,
> ten white roses in one crown, ten red in another, ten pink
> in another. On the panels falling down were written
> different invocations of Our Lady. Last Sunday we had
> the holy hour for the Legion and the girls were so happy
> to be there, I think on account of the decorations.

She ended the letter, her last one of the year, with words that showed she had not lost her sense of humour. 'Do not forget to pray for your old sister. By the way, I'm as ugly as ever and twice as fat.'

10

THE SAGARTS ARE GONE

Things did not get better in 1951. They got worse. This was the year when the Red government made its most determined effort yet to get rid of all foreign missionary influences and to bring the Catholic Church under its control. Yet, despite the constant pressure, Molly never quite sank to the depths of depression that she had experienced the previous year. The spirit in the convent was good, her health had improved, and she discovered that her family had not forgotten her: it was simply that the letters had not been getting through. Her first letter of the year gives some idea of the problems she was facing.

> I am very well, thank God, and working away, but like yourself perpetual worry seems to be the daily dose of suffering. The dearg want na tighe seo [these houses] and as things are very dear we cannot afford to give any presents. Things in the garden are not like they used to be. A lot of the plants are frostbitten and of course are no more use. Some of the yellow rose plants have been transplanted or are about to be in the near future. Then the garden will look poor indeed. But I hope to get some red rose slips in place of them. Perhaps it will look as nice as ever in the summer. Things are hard and getting harder but God's in his heaven, all's right with the world.

The transplanting of the yellow rose plants refers to the arrest of Chinese sisters. The red roses seem to express Molly's hope that some sisters from Europe might come to take their place, a hope that was never to be fulfilled. The communists were now beginning to bring pressure on the nuns to hand over their buildings to the state but Mother Mary of the Cross refused to yield. There was nothing to stop the authorities from simply taking over the convent and school buildings and expelling or imprisoning the nuns; but for some reason that the nuns could not guess, they did not take this step. It was one more sword added to the armoury already hanging over the sisters' heads.

The effect of these difficulties was to draw the community together as never before. Any differences between the sisters were forgotten in this time of common danger:

> We are quite happy and healthy. There never was a better spirit amongst us. For we are up to our neck in it for the Word. The more we are together, the merrier we'll be. We have no time to think of ourselves. Our Holy Mother (the Church) is getting it hot and heavy. Thank goodness, not for the first nor the last time. Something wonderful will be the result of this calling to order.

The months of June, July, August and September were marked by large-scale arrests of priests, nuns and lay leaders. One of the most prominent victims was Father Harold Rigney, rector of the Catholic University in Peking. The University had been taken over by the state the previous year but Father Rigney, now out of a job, was refused an exit visa to leave the country. In his book *Four Years in a Red Hell* he describes his arrest on 25 July 1951. Armed police forced their way into his house and told him, 'You are arrested as an American spy.' They took a medal of Our Lady off his neck and handcuffed his hands behind his back.

> I was then led to the entrance of the compound where I lived and ordered to stand there, facing a group of what seemed like 40 or 50 little children of the parish catechism class with their teacher. These little children knew me and loved me very much. Whenever they saw me, they would run up and surround me, holding my hands and arms, all laughing and talking at the same time.
>
> Now it was so different!
>
> These little creatures had evidently been drilled by the communist police to gather where they did and clap, approving my arrest. Children of lower primary school age, they were too young to hide their emotions.

I shall never never forget that scene!

Handcuffed, I looked at them. Their little faces were distorted and torn by strong conflicting emotions: fear of the cruel communist police; love and sympathy for me, in chains. The poor little creatures were all crying. Some faintly clapped their little hands. Under inhuman pressure, they were forced to act against their finest, deepest, noblest sentiments. My brain was full of thoughts. I thought of what I had heard, how the Chinese communists had forced children to sign death petitions, requesting the execution of their fathers, and wives of their husbands. My heart went out to these tortured little children before me. Their evident sympathy for me consoled me. I blessed them, making a little sign of the cross with my right hand, handcuffed behind my back.

Scenes like this were being repeated all over Peking during those four months. The nuns knew that neither their sex, their nationality nor their religious habit was any guarantee of immunity. Earlier that year, five Canadian nuns running a children's orphanage in Shanghai had been arrested and given prison sentences. The authorities said they had confessed to criminal negligence resulting in the death of 4,000 infants in the orphanage. The community in the Sacred Heart Convent waited for the day when the same thing would happen to them.

* * *

The Legion of Mary was regarded by the regime as the most dangerous of all the organisations working for the Church. In many ways it was a mirror image of the communist party itself. Its praesidia resembled the communist cells, each with a life of its own yet each combining with the others in the service of the organisation as a whole. Its members in China were as highly motivated and dedicated as the communists, willing to work and suffer and, if necessary, die for the cause. Its leaders took special vows: never to miss a meeting, never to refuse a task for the Legion, never to flee even in face of prison or death.

What made it even more dangerous in the eyes of the government was the fact that it was a lay organisation. Each praesidium normally had a priest or nun as spiritual director, but the president and all other officers were lay men or women. The same held true of the whole Legion organisation, right up to the supreme governing body. This meant that the Legion could continue to function in the absence of clergy. This was why the Papal Nuncio, Archbishop Riberi, had encouraged Father Aedan McGrath to form Legion praesidia throughout China in the months before the communist take-over. This was why the new regime singled out the Legion for particular attention in its campaign against Christianity.

As one who had been associated with the founding of the Legion in Peking, Molly was under continual threat of arrest and imprisonment. Nonetheless, she continued to look after her praesidium and to encourage its members. Her letters contain frequent references to its continuing vitality, usually under a code-name: Frank Duff's family or Duff's baby or sometimes, for reasons that remain unclear, Rosewinda.

The first attack on the Legion in Peking was not a success. The authorities unwisely imagined that the junior members would be more amenable to pressure than the adults. They were ordered to attend at the court-house in Peking on a designated day between 10.00 a.m. and 12 noon and to sign a document of repudiation. The form read:

> I, the undersigned, joined the Legion of Mary on . . . [date] and conducted secret counter-revolutionary and evil activities against the Government, the People and Soviet Russia. I hereby resign from the Legion of Mary and promise never to participate in its activities in the future.

An eye-witness of the scene at the court-house (not Molly) later related what happened. Over 1,000 youngsters between the ages of nine and fourteen converged on the building in groups of two and threes. None of them had come to sign the form. They had their mattresses tied to their backs and neat bundles of clothing under their arms. They were prepared to go to prison rather than betray the Legion.

The police were quite unprepared for this response. All they could do was to send the youngsters home again. They had to resort to different tactics, namely, to identify the officers of the Legion, arrest them on fabricated charges, and hope that the rank and file members would fall away once they had been deprived of their leaders.

On 26 August 1951 Molly wrote a letter to her mother, in which she refers to an old sister in the convent who had been given an exit permit and had returned to Europe. In spite of the dangers of her present position, she herself has no desire to leave China:

> The *sagarts* are all gone to Kilmainham [jail]. They will find it very hot and uncomfortable there. That word detachment is very much in vogue nowadays. Perhaps I'll be detached from my old calling. One went away last week. 52 years had been put in working here and she is over 80. At 80 there is only one place I would like to be transplanted to — that is the graveyard.

There is one thing about this letter that makes it unique among all Molly's surviving letters. 'If I write in red ink,' she had said, 'you will know it is very bad.' The letter is written entirely in red.

* * *

Father Aedan McGrath was arrested in Shanghai on 7 September 1951. He was one of a number of priests connected with the Legion of Mary who were rounded up in a concerted action on that same night. In an interview with the magazine *Columbia* he described what happened:

> I was arrested and placed between two policemen who did not allow me to move hand or foot while the others ransacked the room. I was photographed standing in front of a bare table with a picture of Christ the King behind me on the wall — a detail interesting to recount in the light of the fact that afterwards the newspapers throughout the land published a photograph of my arrest showing this table covered with knives, revolvers, grenades and other grisly weapons of war, against a background of pornographic literature and four lightly-clad girls.
>
> In the same papers were cartoons of President Truman stuffing dollars into my pocket — the inference, of course, being that the Legion was being sponsored by imperialist America for her own imperialist designs.
>
> After turning my room upside down for evidence of subversive activity, they hauled me outside to a waiting

jeep and then, accompanied by the full military convoy befitting a notorious criminal, off to jail.

Following two hours of interrogation, I was told to lie down on a concrete floor, a guard armed with a machine gun standing over me. I was not used to concrete floors and I hate machine guns, but believe it or not in about thirty seconds flat I was asleep. On waking, a sudden and extraordinary calm took possession of me, a calm that never left me during the two years and eight months of my imprisonment.

In Peking, Molly was still being harassed by unwelcome visitors. Her life was complicated by an unhelpful newspaper article in Ireland. A reporter from a Cork newspaper visited the house in Little Island and was shown Molly's first letter from communist China. He begged to be allowed print some excerpts from it and Molly's mother unwisely agreed on condition that the sender was not identified. The piece appeared with a rather unfortunate headline and opening paragraph:

'Praties Scarce' in Red China

A letter from an Irish missionary sister in Red-held China — which has just reached Ireland — indicates that food is scarce and that persecution by the Communists has already begun.

She writes:

I was so glad to hear that everyone is on the baker's list. So am I, *Deo Gratias*, but the news is scarce over here and the praties also!

The article went on to quote further extracts which did not in fact say anything about communist persecution but merely stated in general terms that we must expect to suffer in this life. The whole thing occupied no more than a couple of inches in a single column. It was hardly the kind of publicity that was likely to cause shock waves in Chinese government circles, or even come to their attention.

Molly was unaware of the newspaper piece and had long since forgotten about the letter. She was rudely reminded of its existence when she received a visit from three members of the secret police. They forced her to admit authorship of the letter — no very difficult task, since there were few if any other Irish missionary sisters left in China. They went on to accuse her of a two-fold crime of espionage against the state. Her first crime was that she had gathered and spread information liable to damage the People's Republic. Her second crime was that she had been in contact with foreign countries through secret channels and not through the official censor.

The second accusation came as a bolt from the blue. It was true that the offending letter had not been posted in Peking in the usual way. It had been taken out of the country by a missionary leaving China and posted in Hong Kong. It now became clear to Molly not only that every letter she wrote was carefully scrutinised by the censor but that copies of them were kept in the files. They had no copy of her 'praties' letter: therefore, it must have been sent out secretly.

It was a terrifying moment for Molly. In the prevailing climate this could easily be used as material for an arrest and a show trial, followed by imprisonment or even execution. All she could do was answer the charges to the best of her ability. She passed off the remark about praties as a joke and she insisted that the letter had been posted, without mentioning where. After a long and nerve-wracking interview, the policemen rose, gathered their papers and left.

She was not arrested. The round-up of Catholics continued in Peking and throughout the country. Chinese were either executed or sentenced to long terms in prison or in labour camps. Foreign missionaries were imprisoned or expelled. Before long Molly and her companions in the Sacred Heart Convent were the only foreign missionaries still at liberty in China. Day after day, year after year, they waited for the blow that never fell.

* * *

The life of the convent and the school continued in as normal a fashion as possible. Molly's day was divided between praying and teaching. When the school reopened in September 1951 the number of pupils had dwindled to seventy. Four years earlier, there had been 1,000 on the rolls.

Molly wrote her Christmas letters in mid-November. Her sister Enda (Mother Fergus) had been brought back from Africa for health reasons and was now re-assigned to Australia. Molly wrote to her:

The last Sunday of October was a wonderful day. I presume you know it is our special feast. We had three offerings [Masses] as we have every Lord's Day. A lovely hour in the afternoon, all together au pieds de l'hostie [at the foot of the Host]. And a singsong at night. I wonder do you know *Ah, qu'il est bon, le bon Dieu!?* It is a hymn which, if you have not, ask Joannice. It is enough to raise the cockles of anyone's heart.

We pass Sunday like at Châtelets. At night nearly always a song. It helps us forget. This year we have only about 70 chickens. The others got some kind of scour and passed out.

The singsong during the recreation period on Sunday night became a highlight of the week for the nuns. As the world outside grew more hostile and threatening, they turned increasingly to one another for support. They no longer knew who else they could trust. Even the Chinese priests who came to say Mass for them were regarded with some reserve. With so many priests in prison, any priest still at liberty was suspected of having done some kind of deal with the authorities. The nuns would assist at Masses celebrated by these priests but they hesitated to go to Confession to them, unless they were absolutely sure of their good faith. They had heard stories of the secrecy of the confessional being betrayed.

Molly's good humour and irresistible laugh was a priceless asset to the beleaguered community. She was a natural story-teller and she could make the simplest class-room incidents hilarious in the telling. Sometimes the Superior had to ring her little handbell to restore order when the merriment had outstripped what she considered to be the bounds of decorum.

Molly pestered all her family to send her humorous anecdotes that could be used during recreation time. The kind of stories that appealed to her can be gathered from the ones she includes in some of her letters.

I read a good joke yesterday which reminded me of Mrs C. I laughed nearly the whole afternoon.
Husband: 'I don't see any hurry. There's plenty of time for Bessie to get married. Let her wait until the right man comes along.'

Wife: 'I don't see why she should wait that long. I didn't when I was her age.'

Isn't that priceless? Imagine the husband's feelings! It was better than a tonic. It was so like what Mrs C. would say.

On the printed page and to a less innocent generation, these stories may fall rather flat. In the community room, told in Molly's rich Cork accent and accompanied by her infectious laugh and artless comments, they helped to keep the darkness at bay and the light of hope alive a little longer.

Her singing voice was still sweet and true and she enjoyed using it. She would accompany herself and others on a wide variety of instruments — piano, harmonium, guitar, violin, banjo or mandolin. The memory of her that remained longest with the other sisters was her singing of the Irish ballads she had learnt in her youth, *Danny Boy, Mother Machree, The Fairy Tree,* and many others.

One of her favourite songs was still that old standby, *The Kerry Dances*, which meant much more to her now than it had in her younger days.

> Oh, the days of the Kerry dances,
> Oh, the ring of the piper's tune,
> Oh, for one of those hours of gladness
> Gone, alas, like our youth too soon.

As she sang it, the words conjured up images of the old farmhouse at Moord and the big fireplace and the stone floor and the boys and girls lining up for the set dances and Tim Foley playing the accordion and Nora tapping her foot in time to the music and old Mrs Veale presiding over the whole assembly from the depths of her ancient armchair.

> Loving voices of old companions
> Stealing out of the past once more,
> And the sound of the dear old music
> Soft and sweet as in days of yore.

Her Christmas letter to Nancy that year was filled with remembrance of things past. She harked back even earlier than the Moord dances to her childhood Christmasses in Cork, recalling them with nostalgia but without regret.

This is to wish you a very happy holy old-fashioned Christmas. If there are two words I hate, one is 'modern' and the other is 'progress'. It seems to me we've progressed backwards for the last hundred years. And so far back that we are really at about 2000 BC. Is the old planet any happier for all its machines? I don't think so. The old traditions that we had as children when we were happy — how carefree we were when everything fell into our laps. And Dad RIP, who never could do enough for us or give us enough. How unselfish he was. His joy was to make us happy. And his sense of duty — now looking back I can see that he was a model of all virtues.

The other night I was dreaming it was Christmas and all the bustle and hustle of the old days. Dad was hanging up holly and ivy and Mother was making the crib. Those days are gone for ever but the memory is always there and Christmas brings it back. We were all singing — do you remember every one had to 'do her bit', as Dad used say? And when it came to my turn, the bell went. Oh Nance, I was many years and miles from that scene. Another day's teaching was before me. Glad I am to be able to do it. The rookery is very small this year. So say a wee one for us.

11

AN UNEASY TRUCE

Gradually life in the Sacred Heart Convent settled into a new routine. In September 1952 the number of pupils fell to sixty and it seemed as if the school would soon have to close. But in the years that followed the numbers began to rise again and eventually reached 150.

The pupils were mostly children of diplomats accredited to the People's Republic. At first the only countries with embassies in Peking were from the communist bloc but as time went on diplomatic relations were established with many of the neutral countries, mostly from the Third World, and later still with most of the western powers. The personnel of the non-communist embassies were not inclined to send their children to Chinese schools for indoctrination in the thoughts of Chairman Mao. Even though few of them were Catholics, they found the education offered by the Sacred Heart School much more attractive. Among the advantages it offered was its tuition in English offered by native English speakers. It was clear to most diplomats that English was going to be the principal international language of the second half of the twentieth century.

It slowly dawned on the nuns that the reason for their survival was this involvement with the foreign embassies. Clearly the government felt that closing down the convent would cause widespread resentment among those who were in a position to influence opinion all around the world. It was easier to let the nuns continue providing a service for the embassies while making sure that they had as little contact as possible with the local people. Moreover, it was useful to have one convent in Peking which could be shown to gullible foreign VIPs as proof that religious freedom still existed in the People's Republic.

In this way a kind of uneasy truce was established between the government and the nuns. The convent even began to enjoy something approaching diplomatic immunity. Within its wall the nuns had considerable freedom of action. Visits from the police continued but they became rarer and less aggressive as the years passed by. The arrangement was never put into writing or even into words and it could be terminated at any time. Nevertheless, it lasted until the late summer of 1966, by which time the nuns had been for almost fifteen years the only foreign missionaries still at liberty in the People's Republic of China.

Molly now found herself busier than ever. In addition to her mornings and afternoons in the classroom, she was giving evening lessons in music and English. The school began to admit boys to the senior classes, which worried Molly until she found to her surprise that she was quite capable of handling them:

> I like them better than the girls. They are far straighter and do not want to show off or draw your attention all the time. They do their work to the end without lifting their heads. Of course, they are not angels and one finds them sliding down the bannisters more often than walking down the stairs — but boys will be boys.

She discovered that her pupils had a nickname for her: behind her back they called her 'Elephant'. The reason for the nickname was easy to guess. She was not unduly perturbed. By her own admission, her weight had now risen to 'at least 14 stone' but she no longer worried about it as long as she was in good health and spirits. 'Since I entered, every doctor I met told me to take down the weight. I ignored them and I'm able to do my work.' She was pleased to hear that there was some medical opinion on her side.

> Someone told me the doctors are finding out that all the slimming is upsetting the systems no end. When the people stop the dieting, they are developing heart attacks, blood pressure and the rest. And as well as that, bad tempers. So laugh and grow fat.

She may have been wiser than her doctors. If a few extra pounds — or stones — was the price she had to pay for her good humour and easygoing temperament, she felt it was worth it. She got on well with her pupils and they got on well with her.

There was always a lot of laughter in her classroom, usually led by herself. Many of her letters tell of incidents that amused her, mostly centring around the youngsters' imperfect command of English. This was one of the few subjects she could write home about without fear of the censor.

> I am as usual at the same old job and enjoying it with the group I have this year. The other day I told them a story of how a boy learned to control his temper by filling a goblet three times with water and drinking it each time. Then I asked them to write it out. One said the boy filled a bucket three times. He certainly had time enough for his temper to cool down.

One day she asked them to write an essay on 'Our class.' One of them wrote: 'Mother does her level best to be serious but she doesn't always succeed.' It was a tribute that Molly was happy to accept.

* * *

The convent became a kind of island, cut off from the life of the world outside. Molly was often baffled by simple references in letters from her family. Her mother asked her if she would like a present of a book token. 'I have no idea what they are so I cannot tell you,' she wrote back. 'Send one and let us see what it is like.'

The nuns now rarely left the convent. The continuing persecution of the Church in China affected them only indirectly. Sometimes there was a priest to say Mass for them, sometimes there was not. They learned not to ask too many questions.

Molly continued her work with the Legion as long as she could but it soon became impossible for the young Legionaries to come to the convent. The Legion of Mary was now outlawed throughout the country. She asked her mother to send the sad news to a friend. 'Tell him that Frank Duff's baby died and that Fr Aedan could do nothing about it. He is very sorry but as he is on holidays [in prison] at the moment he will be able to forget a little.'

Pius XII declared the year 1954 to be a Marian Year commemorating the centenary of the declaration of the dogma of the Immaculate Conception. Molly was delighted and felt sure that the Blessed Virgin would mark the year by easing the situation in China. Her hopes were soon dashed. A new wave of persecution struck the Church in the spring of that year. The Sacred Heart Convent was spared but her letters indicate that FMMs in other parts of China were less fortunate. (Helen Chap is Hélène de Chappotin, foundress of the order.)

> Helen Chap's kids are getting it rather hard. They are not used to roughing it and find that having to toe the line is not exactly what they like. She sent them to a hard school but it will be all right in the end. Pray for the older ones.

For a long period in the autumn of that year, no priest came to the convent. 'Would you believe that Muire took the last collar on the feast of her name? At the moment it is a regular Lent for the things above.' For the first time in her life she had to miss Sunday Mass and she felt the deprivation very keenly. She began to attend in spirit the Mass offered by a friend of her young days, Father Jim O'Connell, who was now in Australia.

Molly did not go so far as to put Muire into the drawer, but she made her disappointment plain. 'I think not only Muire but all her relations would want their ears seen to. They are as deaf as door nails.' The only consolation was that it was still possible to receive Holy Communion.

> Just to keep you from worrying, I have bread beatha [bread of life] every morning. The boss gives it to me. She is a marvel of strength and keeps all our hearts up. She has a great sense of humour and can see the funny side of everything, even when there is very little of a funny side to see.
>
> Tell J.O'C. that I go in spirit to his morning offering as I am on the same line of longitude. 'Tis nice to know he is as far east as myself. I know he never forgets to put me in the chalice so I'm right there now.

Evidently the last priest to say Mass in the convent had consecrated a large number of hosts which were reserved in the tabernacle and these were distributed to the nuns each morning by the Mother Provincial. In the sacrament and in prayer, Molly found strength:

> It's funny, Nance, but I'm perfectly at peace. I must tell you how. Maybe two weeks ago I felt I had enough of the

112

eternal needle and nearly made up my mind to beat it. I went to say the stations and when I want anything I say the Rosary of the Holy Wounds at each station. So I went on my way and at the second last one I got the idea of cutting *The Imitation*. I fell on the Third Book, chapter 39, verses 1 and 2. 'Await my orders.' I nearly shouted. You read the rest of it. Talk about being told that my job was to obey! So come what may now, sufficient for the day is the evil thereof.

Then I was thinking, if I died, who would forgive my sins? And after it dawned on me. Who really forgives us? I suppose he can work without an instrument for, as the angel said, nothing is impossible with Dia.

By January 1955, Dan was paying a weekly visit, which meant that once again the nuns had Sunday Mass. It is impossible to identify the various Dans and Peters and *sagarts* referred to or to know which ones were able to work openly as priests and which ones only in secret. However, it is clear that the Dan who was coming to the convent in early 1955 was a fugitive. In May Molly wrote:

> Dan did not let us down since but he thinks that he will be going to Gormanstown [prison] for a spell. Most of his pals are on vacation there so he thinks he'll follow suit. He reminds me of Sandow in his youth.

The family would know that Sandow was the nickname of Dan Donovan who commanded the North City battalion of the IRA in Cork. He was one of the men who often spent the night in the O'Sullivan house while on the run.

That year, 15 August, her beloved Feast of the Assumption, brought a special treat.

> I went to 'scrape the skillet' on Saturday. What a relief! I didn't appreciate it when I had Peter at my beck and call, but now we are very thankful for small mercies. Today of course is a posh day. Everything in the garden is lovely, only Charlie Chance is up to his old tricks again. He never lost it. He turns up when you least expect him. I can assure you he is not a welcome guest. Do you remember his doings in Clogheen? He treats Frank's kids [Legion of Mary] in the same way.

Charlie Chance is the police, the name being a charmingly inaccurate reference to Charlie Chan, a Chinese detective who featured in a popular series of Hollywood films in the 1930s.

*　*　*

Molly's love of reading stood her in good stead during the long years of seclusion in Peking. She found as she grew older that her interest in works of fiction disappeared and she preferred the writings and lives of the saints. St Thérèse of Lisieux had been her father's favourite saint and he had often read parts of her autobiography aloud to the family in Little Island. Molly continued to read her and pray to her and she found a new way of enlisting her aid. 'Do you know, I stuck a picture of a *sagart* on the Little Flower's back some time ago and I told her she was to keep him saor [free]. She's done her stuff up to now.'

She found comfort in the life of Thomas More and saw parallels between his England and her China. In both cases, there was an attempt to set up a national church and break the ties with Rome. She felt that her response should be the same as his.

I've lately devoured the life of St Thomas More and now I'm reading his *Wit and Wisdom*. Those books are books which everybody should read nowadays. You know the mill he went through. History is repeating itself. I do not know why I like him so much — after all, he is a Sasanach! . . .

As you know, he was the father of a family but, try as they might, they could not get him to sell his soul. He loved them as few fathers love their children, yet his soul was his chief prize. I do not think I ever cried so much over a book. In one part he tells of the troubles he knew were coming, which he kept to himself so as not to upset his wife. He was a man of iron will with a heart of flesh, not of stone.

Now, because he was faithful, he will go on doing good to the end of time. I hope we'll all be like him if we are put to the acid test. It is not impossible.

Her writing table had a glass top and she used to put pictures of her favourite saints under the glass so that she could keep an eye on them and they on her. When Pope Pius X was canonised in 1954 he was given a place in this private pantheon:

I have him under my glass on my desk. One of his nicest pictures. His eyes follow me everywhere. I've studied his life and I find many things I can imitate. He was a teacher at one period as well as being president of the seminary and administrator of a vacant diocese. He used start his corrections at 11.30 p.m. I don't do that, but when I get tired about half five I feel I can't complain when I look at him.

At the moment I'm reading Charles de Foucauld but I've very little sympathy with him. He's not natural like St Pius, who did the ordinary things of life in a perfect way. It seems to me that he had so much to do that his duty came first and all thought of self was annihilated in that. Anyhow, I talk to him all day long as if he actually heard me. Especially about our holy mother the C. [Church] who is suffering so much at the hands of the 'old boy'.

When John XXIII was elected Pope in 1958, she took to him immediately. He figures constantly in her letters under the name of Seán. News of his election was ignored by the media in China and most Catholics were unaware that they had a new Pope. The nuns were kept informed of the outside world through their contacts with the diplomatic corps and could get copies of foreign newspapers, including Catholic ones. Molly found in Seán a kindred spirit. He was human and humorous and did not take himself too seriously, and these were qualities that she found endearing. She does not mention the fact that he was short and stout, but this probably helped too.

After his death, she added him to her list of saints without waiting for the formality of canonisation. 'He was so simple yet so wise. He knew how to take people, young or old, rich or poor. To use an Irish expression, he had a way with him.' She also admired his sense of duty. 'I ask myself in certain circumstances, "What would he do?" The reply is always the same: obey and do his duty.'

I got a loan of Seán's life and it is wonderful — the one he wrote himself, *The Journal of a Soul*, in diary form. Make yourself a present of it. It is worth its weight in gold. It is very easy to read because of its diary form. It is supernatural from 15 years to 82. The Little Flower was not a patch on him.

He shows the fight he had with himself to become humble. And God did not spare him humiliations. Even in his last job there were some who treated him without a great deal of respect. It hurt him because of whom he represented, not for himself. Nobody has had the effect on me that he has had. I think continually of him, so much so that I've arrived at thinking he's a distraction in my prayers. When I can't read the book I offer it up as a big sacrifice, for it is one.

Sometimes she asked her family to send her books that she had seen mentioned in newspapers. 'I saw there is a book published by Brown and Nolan about Theresa Neumann by an S.J. Maybe you could chance sending it. I know she's dead — perhaps it would do me good.' Theresa Neumann was a Bavarian stigmatic regarded by some as a saint and by others as a charlatan. The book arrived safely and Molly described it as 'an eye-opener'.

Did I tell you Mother sent me a book on Theresa Neumann? I thought it was her life but it was a study of her and, believe me, I came up against things I never thought existed. The author thinks she is a nervous case and not supernatural at all in the doings. If she is a fraud, I wouldn't like to be in her boots. I couldn't imagine anybody wanting to deceive others to that extent. If ever anybody had an idea or desire for ecstasies, I can assure you it would cure them to read it.

Molly concluded that the Little Flower was more to her taste. 'Thérèse of the C.J. [Child Jesus] is a much simpler person and one we can imitate. Hers is an easier way of getting to heaven.' That neatly sums up her attitude to the saints. She looked to them not as interesting historical personages but as models for Christian living, people she could imitate, people she could talk to, people she could follow on the path to heaven.

There was always something essentially simple and humble about her. Raptures or ecstasies were not for her. She did not aspire to the heights of mystical union. She admired the great eagles of the spiritual life but she never felt herself called to be one of them. She admired Pope John because he obeyed and did his duty. She was happy if she could do the same. The words obedience and duty recur constantly and she quotes a song remembered from the days when she sang in *Ruddigore* with The Operatic.

> For duty, duty must be done,
> The rule applies to everyone,
> And painful though the duty be,
> To shirk the task were fiddle-de-dee.

To judge from her letters, her main fault was a streak of stubbornness and self-will. She could be led but she could not be pushed. If she felt she was being pressurised, she dug in her heels. First came an ominous silence; then, if the pressure continued, an outburst of Irish temper. This meant that the unquestioning obedience which at that time was expected of a dutiful nun did not come easily to her. Towards the end of her life, she felt she was beginning to master this trait. She wrote to her mother: 'Do you know that finally I can keep my mouth shut and not blow up at once. But the old stalk is still there. I cannot yet be pushed. I simply stand aside as of yore.'

One self-portrait of her soul survives. It was the custom for every FMM to send an account of herself each year to the Mother General. Molly's letter of 5 January 1949 has been preserved. It was written in the last days before the fall of Peking and it is worth quoting in full. Molly wrote in French. The following is a literal translation:

Very Reverend and Beloved Mother,
Pax Caritas Christi. Another year has passed and I am on retreat. My resolution does not change; it is always the same: humility. Instead of making progress, I think I am falling back. The smallest things upset me. I have too much work to do, that may be the cause. When I am annoyed, I talk to myself out loud. I must make that the subject of my examination of conscience.

This past year has been one of perpetual upheavals, and with war at the gates of the city, one must be ready for whatever God wills. He is the master of all things, and all the lessons that we must learn are taught to us by him.

Mgr Riberi has said that those who stay on here will have a martyr's crown. To remain calm in the midst of all this turmoil there is need of faith. I say to myself that if everyone else leaves, God will stay; and as long as he is in the north of China, I want to stay too.

Mother, it makes me sad to see all the missionaries taking flight before Satan. I am happy that you are leaving us in the hands of God. Not one hair of our heads will fall without his permission. Every day during adoration I read three times the prayer of Mordechai in the formulary and every time I am strengthened.

I am also in charge of the Legion of Mary here. The children are doing great work among the pagans. They are drawing them to Mass and to Father's catechism class. Good is being done in spite of Satan's wrath.

Our province is almost wiped out. It is the province of Christ the King. It may be that his passion is coming to an end. But God will find crosses for his daughters.

Goodbye, Very Reverend and Beloved Mother. Accept my sentiments of filial respect and obedience from your affectionate daughter in Jesus, Mary and Joseph and our father St Francis.

Please bless me.

Mary of St Eamonn, FMM

12

THE LAST PADDY

By the year 1958 the Sacred Heart community were the only foreign missionaries still at liberty in China. Molly herself was to the best of her knowledge the last Irish person in the country. As another Peking winter approached, she wrote to her sister Norrie:

> I believe the temperature is going to fall to 31° below 0 this year. 'There's a good time coming be it ever so far away.' But we will be dressed for it. Nor, you could never imagine wearing so much clothes. We wear padded pants like the cosy cover and have the appearance of a cask of stout, but with all that we are well and happy. Aifreanns are a scarce commodity, about once a week we can afford it. Of course, Iosagán is in our daily diet but we have only a woman cook which is just too bad.
>
> Did you know that Máire was the last Paddy annso [here]? She never expected that bit of good luck. I'm glad for her sake. There are many who wanted that honour and they didn't get it.

Molly had now entered her fifties. She refers sometimes to her advancing age and the approach of death. She had in fact another eight years of life before her, years of routine life in convent and school, years in which nothing much happened. She continued to write home faithfully, once a month to her mother except during Advent and Lent and regularly to her sisters and brothers and a growing flock of nephews and nieces.

It was not always easy to find something to write about. By the time of her death, she had been out of Ireland for thirty years.

Many of the people she knew were dead, others she had forgotten. Some of her own brothers and sisters had only been child en when she left, and she had never met any of the youn;er generation. Her own interests and experiences were comple.cly different from theirs. Furthermore, there were so many things she could not write about freely, including the thing that mattered most to her, her life and work as a nun. Yet somehow or other she kept writing, month after month, year after year, right up to the end, always finding something of interest to say, rarely letting the greyness and grimness of life in Peking show through.

She does not discuss the labyrinthine twists of Chinese politics. 1957 had been the Year of the Hundred Flowers. 'Let a hundred flowers bloom', said Chairman Mao, 'let schools of thought contend'. He humbly admitted that the Party had made many mistakes and was in need of honest and constructive criticism. It turned out that by constructive criticism he meant praise. All those who took him at his word and proceeded to point out the defects in his policies found themselves assigned to labour camps for re-education. The hundred flowers withered. It may have been a genuine attempt at liberalisation which went out of control or it may have been a deliberate ploy to flush the opposition into the open and dispose of them. No-one knows for certain.

The year 1957 had also seen the founding of the so-called Patriotic Church. This was of more immediate concern to Molly. A Patriotic Congress for Catholics was held in Peking at which delegates hand-picked by the government rejected the authority of the Pope and declared that the Church in China must be a Patriotic Church, free of all foreign influence. In the years that followed, bishops and priests were pressurised into supporting the Patriotic Church. Those who yielded were able to keep their churches open, those who resisted were forced to close theirs and often sent to prison or forced labour camps.

To Molly the Patriotic Church was quite clearly in schism and those who supported it were cutting themselves off from the universal Church:

Ár Naomh Mháthair seo-againne [our Holy Mother i.e. the Church] is very sick at the moment. She is tormented with a grievous disease — gangrene. They want to cut off the limb but she is objecting. She would rather die, she says. Maybe the 'doctors' will persuade her to undergo the operation. But I don't think that will save her life. She is too old for such things. Her sons are divided on the subject but I suppose the Lord's will will be done. Don't forget a prayer, for she is a good friend of mine.

The rest of the nuns were of the same mind. They refused to recognise the Patriotic Church and would not allow Patriotic priests to minister in the convent. For a time it was possible to get loyal priests at least for Sunday Mass but the supply began to dry up. One hunted priest stayed for several months in the convent in the guise of a gardener and said Mass every morning for the nuns. Then one day he simply disappeared. They found out afterwards that he had been lured into the street and arrested.

Eventually the nuns found that they must either accept priests who were at least fellow-travellers with the Patriotic Church or else go without Mass and the sacraments altogether. They decided to accept them. There was no doubt that these were validly ordained priests of the Catholic Church and that they had the power to celebrate Mass and administer the sacraments. Their motives for supporting the Patriotic Church were not necessarily selfish. Some of them might genuinely feel that it was better to keep the Church alive in this way than to let it die out, better to bend to the storm than be broken by it. The nuns did not judge them too harshly, but they tried when possible to have a priest who remained loyal to Rome, what Molly called a 'true blue'.

In October 1962 she managed to send out two letters through some unofficial channel, possibly a diplomatic bag. One was to her mother and the other to Nance and in them she could speak more openly than usual. The relief was palpable. To her mother she wrote:

> Oh, for a breath of free air! You have no idea what it is to have to watch every word you say. You know what kind I was. Everything walked straight out of me. Not now. When I'm asked a question my general answer is 'I don't know', whether I do or not. 14 years next January is a long time and there seems to be no end to it.

Her letter to Nance went into more detail. She started by warning her not to mention the letter to anybody because the *dearg* had agents everywhere. Then she went on:

121

We have Mass on an average three or four times a week. Always on Sundays at 8 o'clock for ourselves and the Catholic diplomats who are here. Our sagart is a real true blue. There are lots like him, but many more, including Their Graces, are attacking Seán at the moment. They owe all they have to him or his ancestors and yet they are so ungrateful. Some others are doing time, as you know, and hard labour, and I don't mean 'maybe'. We have confessions every two weeks but we haven't had a sermon since 1954, when our chaplain was sent packing in two hours. Yet we are a happy group, 27 altogether.

I suppose you notice my letters are about everything but annso [here]. They are all opened going out and yours coming in, so be very careful. It is a penance to write a letter because you can't say what you would want to.

A sister buidhe [yellow i.e. Chinese] came back from quod. Nance, we have no idea what suffering is. She went through the mill all right but she was very true to *Dia*. Food was scarce and dear last year but this year there seems to be a greater plenty.

You remember I thought out loud, as you say, but I've learnt silence and to give a sideways answer since the event of the D. One episode to make you laugh. About 12 years ago one day I was being asked a lot of questions by a peeler and I got stuck for an answer, and another old nun turned to me, joined her hands together and raised her eyes and then said, 'Veni Sancte Spiritus' [Come, Holy Spirit]. It was rather serious but I saw the humour of it . . . .

Goodbye, Nance. Hope this letter reassures you that we are all right. The one spot where there is Adoration all day long in this vast empire.

* * *

From 6.30 every morning until 6.00 every evening the Blessed Sacrament was exposed in the convent chapel. The nuns took turns at the kneeler in front of the altar so that there was always somebody there to continue the adoration. This for Molly was the real reason why she was still in China in this convent, 'the one spot where there is Adoration all day long in this vast empire'. Reverence for the Blessed Sacrament had been at the centre of her spirituality ever since she made her first communion. She believed that the hours of silent prayer in the presence of the eucharistic God were a hidden but powerful act of witness and intercession. It was the only justification for the nuns' continued presence in Peking, but it was justification enough and more than enough.

Apart from her prayer, Molly's life had been largely stripped of its religious dimension. Her apostolic work with the Legion of Mary and other groups had ceased. Her daily routine in school was little different from that of any secular teacher. She could teach English or music or biology but she was no longer allowed to teach religion. The only way she could influence those she taught was by the example of her life.

Many of her pupils were in fact deeply influenced by her. After they left the school, they continued to write to her from all parts of the world and she wrote back. On Easter Monday 1962 she wrote to Nancy and told her that it was the eighth letter she had written that day: the previous seven had been to various ex-pupils. That year her class consisted of four Burmese, one Ceylonese, two Yugoslavs, one Moroccan, one Syrian, one Pakistani and one Russian. In addition, she was giving private lessons in English to a number of adults, including two ambassadors' wives.

Though religion was officially forbidden in the classroom, her pupils naturally asked about her life and her beliefs and she asked about theirs. There were Muslims, Hindus and Buddhists among them and Molly found many of her prejudices against these religions disappearing as she came to know more about them. 'I've become very broadminded, Nance, on many things,' she told her sister.

> At the moment I've a fine chance to study Moslems. You know they despise us wholeheartedly because they think we never pray. They think our fast is not strict enough. They begin to fast at seven years. This year during May many of the children fasted, which means nothing from sunrise to sundown, not even a drink of water. They worked all day and kept the fast. Really I felt like a worm beside them.

She found much to admire in the Hindus too, especially their sense of modesty and decorum. During one very hot summer she had two Indian boys in her class who came to school every day in long trousers. She asked them why they did not wear shorts, which were permitted by the school rule. 'The eldest of the two, who is Hindu religion, replied, "Mother, you are a religious and it is not respectful for us to wear short pants where you are." Nance, I said to myself, I only wish the Christians would act like that.'

One of the pupils who kept up contact with her afterwards was a Burmese boy, a Buddhist, who suffered from deafness. She was touched when he wrote to her after his return to Burma and told her that his prayer every night was, 'Please God, send my regards to my parents, Mother Eamonn and the whole world'. At the same time, he was praying to St Martin de Porres to be cured of his deafness. Her comment was, 'In my Father's house there are many mansions.'

When she entered the order, she never expected to become a teacher. She accepted the job only out of obedience but as time went on she enjoyed it more and more. A letter written in the summer of 1964 communicates some of that enjoyment.

> The end of the year with the exams and the rest of the doings is very near. We had a good year, T.G., always enough to do. The children had sports last month and were they excited? They had a great day and we with them. It was a beautiful fine day, not too hot for racing and the other fun. They had a perambulator race. You should have seen them turn those prams in a small space and get away again.
>
> Now we are deaf from piano duets and violins etc. being practised in every corner for the last day. Anyway this makes them buck up and really enjoy their music. I've had the time of my life trying to get a big choir to sing a bolero in time and up to time. They have some very good voices, pure and high. They sing in French and English and they are every shade of colour under the sun from black to white. They all like to sing. Sometimes after years they write back to send the words of such a song. Other subjects they may forget but they don't forget their songs.

During these last years in Peking, the community were more secure financially. Out of twenty-four foreign embassies in the capital, eighteen were sending their children to the convent school. The parents did all they could to make the nuns' lives easier. Presents of food and other necessaries and even envelopes of money seemed to arrive just when they were needed. Molly's last uncensored letter was written in September 1965 to Nance, who was now in the Ursuline Convent in Brecon, Wales.

Well, Nance, Iosagán's wife is very sick and God knows if she will ever recover. She is completely paralysed and her children don't give her any peace. Dan's crowd have disappeared, both the good and the bad. Our Peter is all right now. We have aifreann twice a week, thank God, and all our Rules can be completely followed, so I might as well be in Brecon.

Providence has been a very good provider for us. I suppose you understand it was a big act of abandonment to stay put. But the lilies of the field and the birds of the air are clothed, and our confidence was not deceived. Not very long ago, the oil for the Little Jesus lamp was exhausted. That same morning a gallon of it was handed in at the door, with a 'Pray for me'.

Something which I thought was stranger. One Sunday morning a lady came to the door, handed an envelope to the portress and said, 'De la part de mon mari' (On behalf of my husband). We haven't a notion of who she was nor her husband, but I thought it might be Our Lady on the part of St Joseph. She turned and went down the steps and has never been seen since. Every time we want something, it turns up. So you can imagine our confidence is great.

* * *

The fatal year of 1966, the year of the Cultural Revolution, began with deceptive calmness. The community now numbered twenty-four. Among them were eight foreign nationals, and one of mixed parentage. There had recently been a change in the titles given to members of the order. Only superiors from now on were to be called Mother, all the others were called Sister.

Mother Mary of the Cross, the superior of the province, was Canadian, Mother Olga Sofia, the superior of the convent, was Polish. The other foreigners were Molly, now called Sister Eamonn, from Ireland, Sister Thomas à Becket from Scotland, Sister Sigisbert from France, Sister Joel from Greece, Sister

Notkers from Switzerland and Sister Luigi Antonia from Italy. Sister Fintana was the daughter of an English father and a Japanese mother but had been born in China. The other fifteen sisters were Chinese.

The winter was as cold as usual but the nuns had enough to feed and heat themselves and a little left over to share with the poor people of the locality who came to the door of the convent every day. Some of these ragged men and women were treated with special attention, brought in for a meal and a rest, even allowed to stay for a few days in one of the convent buildings. They were Chinese priests and nuns who were working at labouring jobs or living as vagrants, and who knew that there was always a welcome awaiting them in the Sacred Heart Convent. For a day or two they could be among friends, away from prying and suspicious eyes, they could talk and eat and sleep, they could kneel in silent prayer before the monstrance in the spotless little chapel. Then, refreshed and strengthened, they slipped away as quietly as they had come into the snowy streets outside.

There were other visitors to the convent who came more openly. Diplomatic relations had been established between the United Kingdom and the People's Republic and there was now a British embassy in Peking. A number of English children were attending the school, two of them in Molly's class. More important, the nurse attached to the embassy was an Irishwoman, Rita Hennessy from Ennis in Co. Clare, and she came to the convent every Sunday for Mass. It was a great joy for Molly to see an Irish face and hear an Irish voice and ask a thousand questions about the country she had not seen for thirty years.

Those thirty years had done nothing to lessen her love for her native land. She did not regret the giving up of home and family but she never ceased to feel it. 'The first sacrifice in our life is only the beginning', she once wrote. 'It continues every day to the end of the chapter.' She looked forward as eagerly as ever to the letters from her family in Ireland, from Nancy in Wales from Pam in England, from Enda in Australia. Her mother was now eighty-four years of age but she continued to write regularly and send all the news about her children and her twelve grandchildren.

Molly wrote to all of them. Her nephews, John and Patrick Quinlan, were confirmed together on 16 May 1966. Each received a letter of good wishes and good advice from Auntie Molly. Another nephew, Eamonn Barry, had begun to study for the priesthood in Carlow College. Molly not only wrote several letters to him, she wrote about him to other members of the family, making no attempt to conceal her pride. Her generation of the family had produced three nuns but no priest. The next generation was about to repair the omission.

The summer term ended as usual with a flurry of sports and concerts and exams. The young people said their goodbyes to their teachers, some of them for good, others just until the new term began in September. The nuns tidied up the empty school, sweeping out the classrooms, putting away books and music and instruments and leaving everything in readiness for the beginning of the new school year. Then they settled down for two months of comparative rest, with only a few private pupils to disturb the lassitude of a Peking summer.

Molly wrote her last letter on 17 July. It was to her mother.

> The heat set in two days ago and we're stewing in our own juice. Everybody you meet has a hanky in her hand, wiping her face or hands. Sometimes we burst out laughing, it looks so funny. Now we're having what I call the annual Turkish bath. The funny thing is that the temperature is not very high but it's like heavy foggy November weather at home, without a breath of air. The nights are as heavy as the days. We are doing a spot of work in the morning, not very much. I've only five but it's enough for the summer.

Molly had one more opportunity to send a message to her mother before the end. It happened in an unexpected way. On the morning of the 26 July, Nurse Hennessy came to the convent with a visitor for Sister Eamonn. She was Eileen O'Rourke, a Corkwoman who was making a conducted tour of China and had just heard that there was a fellow Corkonian in the Sacred Heart Convent. Molly was in class at the time but when she heard about the visitor she gave the pupils some work to do and made for the parlour to meet her.

In an article later written for *The Sunday Press*, Eileen described Molly as a plump, fresh-complexioned woman who looked younger than her fifty-nine years. Molly was thrilled to meet somebody from her native city and an animated conversation followed, conducted mainly in whispers. Eileen had to describe all the changes that had taken place in Cork during the last thirty years and to promise to send some photographs of the city when she got home.

Every now and then when the talk grew too loud, Molly would point to the ceiling and warn that there could be microphones concealed in the room. She said that when the nuns went to Confession, they walked in the garden with the priest to ensure privacy.

Eileen asked about the priest and was told that he was a Chinese Franciscan who said Mass every Sunday at 8.00. Occasionally he failed to turn up and on the following Sunday no explanation was given or asked for. Was he an adherent of the Patriotic Church? Molly said they didn't know and were afraid to ask.

Before leaving, Eileen was brought to see the convent chapel and say a prayer. She asked Molly if she could bring back any message to her mother. Molly gave her a medal with a Chinese inscription but said she was afraid to give her a letter. She had heard too many stories of travellers having their baggage searched at customs for incriminating documents. Instead she asked Eileen to go and see her mother when she got to Cork and give her a verbal message. 'Tell her', she said, 'I am fit and well, as fat as ever, and still singing.'

At the door of the convent, Molly took her by the hand and prayed that God would keep her safe on her long journey home. Then she embraced her and said, 'You won't forget to give my message to my mother? Tell her how fit I am.' She stood on the steps of the convent waving until they had turned the corner of the street.

13

THE RED GUARDS

The Great Proletarian Cultural Revolution of 1966 was one of the most bizarre events of modern history. Like the Hundred Flowers episode, it was obscure in origin, unclear in motivation and devastating in effect. But the devastation it wrought was on an incomparably vaster scale. For a period of some ten years, the most populous nation on earth found itself in a state of continuous turmoil. Law and order disintegrated, tradition was trampled under foot, the oldest civilisation in human history was systematically reduced to rubble. The administration of the country was taken over by mobs of juvenile misfits and malcontents. Communism was replaced by hooliganism. Chaos became an end in itself.

Mao was still undisputed ruler of China, but he was growing old and like every ageing despot was becoming suspicious of those who might aspire to take his place. He found it easy to convince himself that they were unworthy to succeed him, that they were corrupted by ambition, greedy for power, softened by years of easy living. The pure hard flame of revolutionary fervour that burnt in him had no place in their bourgeois hearts. He looked at those around him and saw few that he could trust.

He turned instead to the younger generation. In the youth of China he saw the hope of the future. They had not yet lost their enthusiasm and their generosity. There was still time to mould them according to his ideals. He could put them through a revolutionary experience that would purify them and motivate them and inspire them. He could turn them into an army that would sweep away everything that was old and settled and comfortable. He could build a new and greater China that would think his thoughts and speak his words and honour him as he deserved.

Something like that must have been going through his mind as he planned his last great campaign, the Cultural Revolution. He began it by an attack on the Four Olds: old culture, old thinking, old habits, old customs. Students and other teenagers were called on to lead the attack against the Four Olds and to join the new revolutionary movement, the Red Guards. During the summer of 1966 they were given free food and free travel so that they could make the pilgrimage to Peking and sit at the feet of the Chairman. Day after day, they packed the vast square in the centre of the city, wearing their red armbands, chanting their slogans and brandishing their copies of the Little Red Book, *Quotations from Chairman Mao Tse-tung*. A true Red Guard had the Chairman's words about revolution imprinted on his or her heart.

> A revolution is not a dinner party, or writing an essay, or painting a picture, or doing embroidery; it cannot be so refined, so leisurely and gentle, so temperate, kind, courteous, restrained and magnanimous. A revolution is an insurrection, an act of violence by which one class overthrows another.

The Red Guards returned to their homes in towns and villages throughout China and waited for the signal. It came in August. It was as though a monster were suddenly unleashed. Mobs of Red Guards rampaged through the streets, searching out and destroying anything that was old or venerable or traditional, anything that showed beauty or craftsmanship, anything that spoke of the culture of a bygone age. Those who were linked or tainted with the Four Olds were shown no mercy. Teachers, writers, artists, those whose homes or possessions showed signs of education or good taste, were treated as enemies of the people. Their houses were ransacked, their goods destroyed, they themselves were beaten up or thrown into prison. Many died from the treatment they received.

The most fanatical and brutal of the Red Guards were those of lowest intelligence and ability. Teenage boys and girls who were social misfits, failures in school, unemployed and unemployable, who had been dabbling in petty crime and vandalism and in a normal society would be attracting unfavourable attention from the police, now found themselves in a position of almost absolute power. They could avenge themselves on all those whose success was a reproach to their own failure. The teachers who belittled them, the educated who looked down on them, the wealthy who provoked them to envy, could be dragged down to their own level. A licence for violence and vandalism, a blank cheque for robbery, had been put into their hands and they were going to use it to the full.

Among the targets of the campaign were all forms and manifestations of religion. Religion was filled with the spirit of the Four Olds and must be destroyed. Christianity was not the only target. Mosques were attacked, Buddhist shrines defaced, Confucian temples destroyed, Taoist tablets and altars demolished. The attack on the Catholic and Protestant churches was only one element in a nationwide pattern of destruction.

Tuesday, 24 August was the day set for the onslaught on the Christians. On that day, according to a South China newspaper, all the churches in Shanghai 'were stripped of crosses, statues, icons, decorations, and all church paraphernalia by the revolutionary students, wearing Red Guard armbands and determined to eradicate all traces of imperialist, colonial and feudal regimes'. The same thing was to happen in Peking.

*   *   *

The summer tutorials were held as usual in the Sacred Heart School on the morning of Tuesday, 24 August 1966. The children came at the normal time, attended their classes and went home again for their lunches. The nuns had their own lunch in the convent refectory.

The afternoon was largely free, as it was still holiday time. In the chapel, the Blessed Sacrament was exposed and a sister was kneeling in adoration before the altar. Of the others, some were in their rooms, some in the garden, some doing various jobs around the house. Sister Thomas à Becket was in one of the classrooms, preparing her books for the new term which was due to start at the beginning of September. She could hear Molly in another classroom at the same task, singing away to herself as she so often did.

Some time in mid-afternoon the doorbell rang. The sister portress opened the door and was confronted by a group of Red

131

Guard leaders, wearing blue Mao-style jackets and caps and red arm-bands. They told her that the religious emblems on the outside of the convent were offensive and would have to be removed. In particular, they demanded that the nuns should immediately take down the large statue of the Sacred Heart over the front door. Mother Mary of the Cross was sent for and she explained that the statue was large and heavy and embedded in concrete, and therefore very difficult to move. They answered, 'If you can't do it, we will. At the very least, it will have to be covered up'. Then they left, but there was no doubt in anyone's mind that they would be back.

Mother Mary of the Cross realised that the situation was difficult, but they had been in difficult situations before and survived. She was hopeful that the influence of the embassies would once again avert the danger that threatened them. She did not alert the rest of the community immediately. The daily exposition ended at 6.00 p.m., the Blessed Sacrament was returned to the tabernacle, and the nuns went to the refectory for their evening meal. Before the evening prayers at 8.00 p.m. she asked the nuns to come to the community room and briefly outlined the situation for them. Then they all went to the chapel and began to say the rosary together.

They were still at their prayers when they heard the doorbell ringing again, this time accompanied by shouts and other noises that suggested a large crowd outside. Mother Olga Sofia went to the door, accompanied by a Chinese ex-novice called Yana who lived in the convent. They opened the door and were brushed aside by a crowd of Red Guard leaders, who marched in and took possession of the entrance hall.

Hearing the commotion, Mother Mary of the Cross told the nuns to go upstairs to their rooms. They did so without hindrance from the intruders, who let them pass and then sat on the stairs. They were waiting for reinforcements, which were not long in arriving. Suddenly, a huge mob of Red Guards came surging up the steps and in through the front door, shouting and screaming and brandishing a large variety of weapons, knives, hatchets, scissors, hammers, whips. They went rushing through the halls and corridors of the convent, up the stairs, into the rooms, opening closed doors, breaking down locked ones, destroying anything that stood in their way and filling the whole house with the sound of their blasphemies and obscenities.

With considerable presence of mind, Mother Olga Sofia ran back to the chapel to protect the sisters' greatest treasure. She opened the tabernacle and took out the ciborium that held the consecrated hosts. Looking around for a hiding place, her eye fell on a refuse bin, filled with old newspapers and other rubbish. She thrust the ciborium into the bin and covered it with pieces of waste paper, hoping and praying that none of the marauders would think of looking there.

Upstairs, the Red Guards were dragging the terrified nuns from their rooms and herding them down to a large room on the ground floor. On the way down, they kicked and hit the nuns repeatedly and showered them with insults. The only ones left upstairs were Mother Mary of the Cross, who was forced to stay in her room accompanied by Sister Marguerite, an eighty-three-year-old Chinese nun. Mother Mary, who was seventy-six herself, was treated as roughly as the others. One of the Reds attacked her with a whip, lashing her across the face with such force that her eye was almost knocked out. She noticed that the others seemed angry at this and shouted at the one with the whip. It would seem that they had been given leave to beat the foreign nuns and insult them as much as they liked but not to inflict permanent injury on them.

They then began to torture Mother Mary in a different way. They brought a large statue of the Blessed Virgin into her room and started to attack it with hammers and hatchets. 'Look at your mother', they shouted as they knocked off the head and hands and covered the floor with fragments. Having demolished the statue, they turned on the crucifix that stood on her desk and treated it in the same way. This went on all through the night until her room and all its contents were completely wrecked.

In the large room downstairs, the other sisters were being entertained in the same fashion. Statues, crucifixes, pictures and other religious objects were collected from all over the convent and brought into the room, where they were broken to pieces in front of the sisters' eyes. The Guards spattered the broken fragments with red paint and dumped them into the sisters' laps, until their white habits were streaked and stained with red. They showed special hatred for the crucifixes, throwing them on the ground and trampling on them to show their contempt. They tried to make some of the nuns walk on the crucifixes too but without success.

After this, the sisters were made to go into the chapel and sit on the floor. They had to look on helplessly while the Reds embarked on an orgy of destruction. Altar, tabernacle, crucifix, statues, stations of the cross, candlesticks, vases, sanctuary lamp, everything that could be destroyed was destroyed. This was the chapel that the sisters had cared for so lovingly all down the years, polishing the metal, waxing the woodwork, mending the threadbare vestments and altarcloths, conjuring up elaborate decorations of flowers and draperies for the great feasts of the Church. The group of elderly women, most of them in their sixties and seventies, sat there through it all, weeping quietly to themselves. Their only consolation was that the Reds had not yet found the ciborium.

Eventually, the long night drew to an end and the light of a new day came into the wrecked convent. The nuns were told they could go to the refectory for some food. The sister who did the cooking for the community was allowed to serve them a simple meal. While she was preparing it, Mother Olga Sofia managed to retrieve the ciborium from the refuse bin. She gave the hosts to the sister cook and asked her to try and distribute them to the nuns along with the other food. The room was filled with Red Guards, jostling and shouting, and it was difficult to distribute the hosts without being detected. The cook gave them to the nearest nun, who was Sister Thomas à Becket, and asked her to swallow some and pass the rest on. She did so and passed the remainder on to Molly, who was next to her. Molly noticed one of the Reds looking at her suspiciously and in a panic she crammed all the hosts into her mouth and succeeded in swallowing them. It was her last Communion.

After their breakfast, they were ordered to go to bed. The foreign nuns were separated from the Chinese and put into a dormitory, with one or two Guards near each bed. They were told that they could sleep but must not attempt to speak or communicate with one another in any way.

* * *

The next few days passed like a kind of bad dream. Looking back on them afterwards, the sisters found it hard to remember on which days the various events happened and in what order. From Wednesday to Sunday, they never had a moment's privacy or quiet. The Red Guards came in relays, vying with one another in their threats and insults and physical abuse, but always stopping short of serious injury in the case of the European sisters.

The treatment of the Chinese sisters seems to have been subject to no restraint. As they were kept apart from the foreigners, it was hard to know exactly what was happening to them. All day Thursday the foreign nuns were kept in the dormitory and could not see what was happening outside. But from the noise it was evident that the Chinese sisters were being brought out on the steps in front of the convent, to be jeered and beaten by the crowd. During a momentary lull, Mother Olga Sofia recognised the voice of one of the sisters saying the single word, 'Jesus'.

The next day, Friday, they were brought out on the steps again and this time the foreign sisters were brought out with them. They could not speak to the Chinese sisters but they could see the marks of their ill-treatment plainly on their faces. They were told that they were about to be put on trial and that The People would be their judges.

The area in front of the main door, approached by a flight of a dozen steps, made a suitable stage or platform where the accused could stand in full view of the crowd. A system of microphones and loudspeakers had been rigged up so that everyone could hear the crimes with which they had been charged. It was not thought necessary to make any arrangement for the accused to reply to these charges. They would not have been accused if they had not been guilty.

Before the trial began, Red Guards pulled the veils and head-dresses off the nuns. It was the first time they had ever appeared in public without their head-dresses since they had entered the convent. They were forced to bow their bodies and remain in that position while a long harangue against them was delivered over the public address system. Then they were made kneel with their foreheads on the ground for the reading of the indictment.

According to the Chinese newspapers, the nuns were accused of the following crimes:

> They secretly colluded with a number of counter-revolutionaries in the Catholic churches in Peking, Hopei, Shansi, Inner Mongolia and Harbin, undertook espionage of information about China, printed reactionary documents, fabricated and spread rumours, instigated

counter-revolutionaries to engage in plots to create riots, and committed acts of sabotage seriously detrimental to China's sovereignty.

The reading of the indictment was greeted with fury by the onlookers. There was no doubt that the verdict of The People, as represented by this particular crowd, was 'guilty'. The sentence was not due to be passed yet. Instead, the nuns were brought back into the convent to be interrogated and given an opportunity to make a full confession of their crimes.

The Chinese and foreign sisters were again separated. The foreigners were put into different rooms, each one with a group of Red Guards who shouted abuse and threats at them for several hours until they were hardly able to think. Then they were each subjected to a private trial before a representative of the police who tried to convince them that they were guilty of a wide variety of counter-revolutionary activities. Finally, in the last stages of exhaustion, they were allowed to go to bed.

* * *

No public event took place on the following day, Saturday. The foreign sisters were still forbidden to speak to one another and were completely separated from the Chinese sisters. The convent was full of Red Guards, who continued to devise various means of insulting and menacing the nuns.

They would thrust their faces right into the nuns' faces and shout, 'You are a pig' or 'You are a dog'. They would put a pistol to a nun's head and pull the trigger, roaring with laughter when the gun turned out to be unloaded. As all the religious objects had been destroyed, they started smashing the bookcases and tearing up the books.

One of them said to Mother Olga Sofia, 'Do you love Chairman Mao?' She answered, 'I am a Christian and I do love Chairman Mao. I love the Chinese people very much. In fact, I love you too.' This discomfited the youth and he mumbled, 'We don't love you. We hate you'.

It gradually became apparent that one of the foreign nuns was being picked out for special persecution. That one was Molly. There seem to have been two main reasons for this. One was her association with the Legion of Mary. The Legion had long ago ceased to have any public existence but it was still convenient for the authorities to invoke its name as an evil counter-revolutionary agency. It was useful to have a scapegoat upon which the blame for many of the government's own mistakes could be fastened. It provided an object of hate on which the people could vent their frustrations. Molly had been one of the founders of the Legion in Peking and was a marked woman ever afterwards.

The other reason was a rather strange one. One of her companions wrote afterwards:

> I was her next-door neighbour during the whole four days of our imprisonment in Peking. From time to time we were able to whisper a word or two. She was very patient, smiling at the insults addressed to her. She received a bigger share than we, because she was fairly well built. I admired her patience greatly.

Molly was now fifty-nine years of age and was the youngest of the foreign nuns. Her appearance was variously described by the others as 'robust' or 'well built'. She herself was more forthright in her description. 'I'm as fat as a fool', she told her sister Pam with disarming candour. It made her a natural target for blows and insults. The Red Guards had apparently been warned that none of the foreigners must die or be seriously injured because it would provoke unfavourable reaction abroad. Molly seemed to be the one least likely to succumb under their attacks so she got more than her fair share of kicks and blows.

She got more than her fair share of insults too. One of the regular accusations made against missionaries in China was that they grew fat at the expense of The People. In the past, they had even been accused of killing babies in their orphanages and eating them. All these accusations were thrown against Molly. 'Fat Pig' became the Reds' normal way of addressing her. 'Fat Pig, Fat Pig' they would shout and chant at her for hours on end. They wrote 'Fat Pig' on the walls of her room, on her white habit, on her headdress.

Molly responded with surprising equanimity. She had long ago come to terms with her rotundity. One of the sisters overheard a Guard jeering at her and saying, 'You're too fat!' Molly answered cheerfuly, 'That's true.' Years ago she had adopted 'Laugh and grow fat' as her motto. She saw no reason to change it now.

* * *

Early on Sunday morning the foreign nuns were told they were going to be expelled from the People's Republic and were ordered to pack a small suitcase with a few belongings for the journey. They received the news with mixed feelings. Having persevered for so many years through so many difficulties, it was sad to have to leave at this late stage of their lives. But it was an immense relief to know that the ordeal of the last four days was coming to an end and that they were not going to be killed or imprisoned.

They packed their bags and waited for further information. There was some doubt about Sister Fintana, who was born in China but had an English father. She regarded herself as English, was regarded as English by the other sisters, and could hardly speak a word of Chinese. No-one would tell her whether she was to go or stay, but she packed her suitcase and waited like the rest.

During the afternoon a particularly vicious gang of Red Guards selected a few of the sisters for their entertainment. Molly was one of the victims. They were made to run the gauntlet up and down the stairs with their suitcases in their hands while their tormentors shouted 'Hurry up! Hurry up!' and beat them on the feet and legs with bamboo canes. This was kept up until the sisters were collapsing with exhaustion. Only then were they allowed to crawl back to their rooms.

Around 6.00 p.m. the foreigners were told to come down and assemble in the chapel. The nine sisters stood there among the wreckage and listened to the sound of an angry crowd assembling outside the convent. They wondered what fresh ordeals might lie ahead. Then they were ordered to go out on to the front steps. As they walked towards the main door, Sister Fintana was stopped and told she had to stay. She stood there with her suitcase in her hand and watched the others pass her by, unable even to say goodbye to her. It was a moment of extraordinary poignancy. They never saw her again.

From the top of the steps, the eight looked out on a vast sea of faces. They were told to bow down once again while The People passed sentence on them. There followed a number of denunciations of the nuns and their work, broadcast through the loudspeakers. According to the Chinese media, these were delivered by 'revolutionary people and victims trampled underfoot and oppressed by the reactionary missionaries.' Then the sentence was announced in a long and rambling diatribe. The eight nuns were sentenced to be expelled from the People's

Republic of China. The sentence was to be carried out immediately.

The sisters were led down the steps and then pushed through the tightly packed crowd to the jeeps that were waiting to bring them to the train. No attempt was made to clear a path for them and they had to endure kicks and blows from all sides as they made their way down the street. They were loaded into the jeeps and brought quickly to the railway station. There was no demonstration at the station and the nuns were quietly put on board the train that was to bring them to Hong Kong.

14
JOURNEY'S END

As the train left the station in Peking for the long journey southwards, the nuns on board were unaware of the interest that the world was taking in their plight. The alarm had been raised on Thursday morning when the embassy children going to school had found the building in the hands of the Red Guards. Foreign correspondents in Peking picked up the story and it was carried that evening by Japanese radio. The next day it was taken up by the broadcasting media in Europe and America and on Saturday it was on the front pages of newspapers throughout the world.

The first reaction of most people was astonishment. Astonishment first of all at the behaviour of the Red Guards, who up to then had scarcely been heard of in the West. Astonishment also at the news that there was still a Catholic convent and school open in China and staffed by both foreign and Chinese nuns. For years the nuns of the Sacred Heart Convent had avoided any kind of publicity, in case it would endanger their work. As a result, most people believed that all the foreign missionaries in China had been either expelled or imprisoned.

The second reaction was concern. It was impossible to obtain accurate news from Peking about what was actually happening at the convent. Foreign correspondents in the city were unable to get access to the building. The news reports in the Chinese media were of little use, consisting mainly of long catalogues of crimes supposedly committed by the sisters. The only thing certain was that the nuns were in great danger. Prayers for their safety were offered up in churches and convents all over the world.

In Little Island a family reunion was taking place. 1966 was the sixtieth anniversary of Nora's wedding and her children decided to celebrate the event on 28 August. All the family except Molly were expected, their first time together in more than thirty years. The other two nuns were coming back from their convents, Nance from Wales, Enda from Australia. Pam was coming from England, Barry, Kitty and Norrie from their homes in Ireland. Eamonn and his family were living with Nora at Little Island and farming the land.

The news from Peking turned a joyful occasion into a long agony of waiting and worrying for the O'Sullivan family. The first confused reports were ominous, telling of mass rallies outside the convent and public humiliations of the nuns. Then came word that they were to be expelled from China and the family's hopes rose again. It even began to look as though Molly might be able to join them at Little Island and make the reunion complete.

* * *

The journey from Peking to Canton lasted more than forty hours. The eight nuns were put into two compartments, four in each. A large contingent of Red Guards travelled on the train with them to make the journey as unpleasant as possible. They came in and out of the compartments constantly, shouting at the sisters, calling them names and forbidding them to speak to one another. But there was no more physical violence. Since the sisters would shortly be seen by the outside world, it was not desirable that they should have any visible marks of recent ill-treatment.

The worst moments came whenever the train stopped at a station. All along the route, mobs of Red Guards had been assembled on the platforms of the stations where the train was to stop. As soon as it came to a halt, they pressed up against the windows of the carriage, shouting anti-imperialist slogans and making threatening gestures. All those young faces distorted by hatred and young fists clenched in rage were a frightening sight for the sisters, protected from them only by the width of a pane of glass. They feared that at any moment the mob might board the train and attack them, a fear which was renewed at every halting place on the 1500-mile journey.

The Guards travelling with them began to show occasional

glimpses of humanity. The nuns noticed after a while that they were taunted and insulted only when there were two or three of the Guards present, as if they felt that they had to prove their revolutionary fervour to one another. Some of them, especially the girls, would seize the opportunity for a kind word or gesture when alone with the nuns. One of the girls came into the compartment where Mother Olga Sofia was and said to her with tears in her eyes, 'You are very good'. Then she said to the others, 'You are all very good', and embraced them quickly before she left.

Mother Mary of the Cross was in the same compartment as Molly. She related afterwards how they prayed together all the time, frequently renewing their religious vows and laying particular stress on the words, 'I offer myself as a victim for the Church and for souls, especially for China'. They prayed above all for the members of the community who had been left behind and who had no prospect of liberation to look forward to.

All through that long Monday, the train continued its journey southward. Molly seemed to be well enough, though like the others she was exhausted from the strain and the lack of sleep. She even managed an occasional humorous remark to keep her companions in good spirits. On Monday night they all dozed a little where they sat until the first light of Tuesday came into the carriage and woke them again. As dawn brightened into full day, the others noticed that Molly was looking very pale and ill but they were not unduly alarmed. Another day or so should see them all in Hong Kong where proper care and medical attention were awaiting them.

The train arrived in Canton about 2.00 p.m. on Tuesday. The nuns were taken to a hotel where they were treated well and offered a substantial meal, their first proper meal in six days. Molly was showing signs of fever and was unable to eat anything. They were given comfortable rooms in the hotel for the night but Molly slept very little.

On Wednesday morning they were taken to the station and put on the train for the three-hour journey to Hong Kong. Molly was now seriously ill. Her temperature was taken. It was 105°. She was given some pills and an injection and the others tried to make her comfortable. She was still conscious as the train approached the railway bridge at Lo Wu and began to slow down.

* * *

The small river at Lo Wu marked the boundary between China and the British colony of Hong Kong. The railway bridge that spanned it was about 200 yards long and was covered with a corrugated iron roof. In those days of tension between East and West, it was regarded as a kind of no-man's-land. The train bringing food and other supplies to Hong Kong used to stop on the Chinese side and any passengers on board were made to get off and walk across the bridge. The train would follow them and they were allowed to board it again on the Hong Kong side to complete their journey into the city.

By midday on Thursday quite a crowd was waiting on the platform on the Hong Kong side. Though nothing was known for sure, it was thought likely that the expelled sisters would be on that day's train. Priests, nuns, policemen, medical personnel, reporters and cameramen waited for the train to arrive and the passengers to disembark. The presence of a large crowd of Red Guards on the far side of the bridge strengthened their belief that the missionaries were on their way. The man in charge of the station security that day was Superintendent Matt O'Sullivan of the Hong Kong Police, a native of Co. Cork.

The Canton train arrived soon after midday and stopped at the usual point. After a pause, the watchers on the Hong Kong side saw eight nuns in black veils and white habits getting off the train. They were carrying suitcases in their hands. The Red Guards immediately started chanting slogans and waving their fists at the sisters. Many of them were carrying brooms in their hands with which they threatened to strike them.

The nuns started to walk from the train but almost at once one of them collapsed and lay motionless on the ground. Some of the others tried to help her but were prevented by the Red Guards. They were forced to stand in line while photographs were taken and the shouting and insults continued. Then the Red Guards started to make sweeping movements with their brooms. The symbolism was evident. They were sweeping the dirt out of their country.

Once again the sisters began to walk towards the bridge. They tried to help the nun who had fallen but she was too weak to move herself and too heavy for the others to carry. The people on the other side could only look on helplessly while the nuns appealed for someone to come to their aid. After some moments of indecision, a few soldiers lifted the prostrate woman and threw her face downward on to a nearby trolley. It was a rough trolley with iron handle and wooden wheels, used for transporting heavy baggage. With some difficulty, a couple of the nuns managed to get it moving and pushed it laboriously the 200 yards to freedom.

As soon as they had stepped off the bridge on the other side, the nuns found themselves once again surrounded by a shouting, heaving crowd. This time it was a friendly crowd. Reporters called out questions, cameramen jostled for angles, friendly arms reached out to support them, friendly hands grabbed for their suitcases, still scrawled with insults. Superintendent O'Sullivan made for the trolley and with the help of some others carried it as if it were a stretcher to the waiting-room. Someone told him it was the Irish nun he was carrying.

In the waiting room, some refreshments had been prepared for the nuns. Molly revived a little when she was given something to drink. She looked up and saw a broad Irish face beaming down on her while a broad Irish accent identified the owner as Matt O'Sullivan from County Cork. She smiled. The Mother Provincial of the Franciscan Missionaries of Mary in Hong Kong came forward with a telegram. It read: 'Welcome back. All delighted you are out. Love from the whole clan. Mam.' She smiled again.

An ambulance was sent for and as soon as it arrived Molly was carried into it, clutching the telegram in her hand. She was accompanied in the ambulance by Mother Mary of the Cross, who was also in a very weak condition. They were brought to St Teresa's Hospital where they were put to bed and given a medical examination. Their condition seemed comfortable and there was thought to be no cause for alarm.

During the night, Molly's temperature suddenly rose. The doctors were sent for but they could do nothing to bring it down. The chaplain came and gave her the last rites of the Church. She was able to make her Confession to him but was too weak to receive Communion. He then gave her the Sacrament of Extreme Unction, anointing her eyes, ears, nose, mouth and hands with the holy oil.

Word was sent to the FMM convent that she was sinking fast. The Mother Provincial and a number of the nuns came over to the hospital to be with her at the end. They said the prayers for the dying around her bed and for a while she was able to join in. All the time she held in her hands a rosary beads that had been given to her on her arrival in the hospital and that had come from the Mother General in Rome. Her own rosary beads had been taken from her in Peking.

Towards morning she grew weaker and was no longer able to say the prayers aloud but she continued to move her lips for a time. Then even that ceased and only her breathing showed that she was still alive. She died very quietly and very peacefully at about 6.45 a.m. It was Thursday, 1 September 1966.

* * *

The expulsion of the nuns and the death of one of them caused reactions of anger and outrage throughout the world. Photographs of the nuns arriving at Lo Wu and Sister Eamonn being pushed along on the luggage trolley were reproduced in all western newspapers. The accusations made by the Red government did not need to be refuted in words. The scene at Lo Wu said it all. No-one could believe that these eight ageing women were dangerous conspirators who had been plotting the overthrow of the People's Republic.

The reaction was particularly strong in Ireland. The Irish government had no representative in Peking but they sent a strong protest through their embassy in London. The protest was rejected by the Chinese government and returned by post to the embassy.

The reaction was strongest of all in Molly's native city and within days of her death moves were being made to have her remains brought back to Ireland. A committee was formed under the chairmanship of the Lord Mayor of Cork, Alderman Seán Casey, and permission was obtained from the Hong Kong authorities to have her remains exhumed from the cemetery where they had been buried.

The plane bearing the coffin arrived at Cork airport on Thursday 29 September. Among those who waited on the tarmac was Molly's eighty-four-year-old mother, standing erect between two of her daughters, with the rest of her family around her. The funeral procession left at 4.30 p.m. for the short journey to the city. From Ballyphehane on, crowds lined all the streets, children in school uniforms, workers returning from offices and factories. The procession stopped and re-formed at the City Hall.

The O'Sullivan brothers and nephews walked immediately behind the hearse, followed by the Lord Mayor and the City Councillors in their robes of office. Behind them marched 200 pupils from St Aloysius's School, where Molly had received her secondary education. As they drew near St Patrick's Church, the crowds were so dense that they spilled on to the roadway and the cortège could barely pass.

The coffin lay in state that night in St Patrick's, the church where Molly had been baptised. The next day, the Bishop of Cork, Dr Cornelius Lucey, presided at Solemn Requiem Mass. Nance describes the scene:

> There was a feeling of joy, great joy and not sorrow in this ceremony. The Bishop gave the solemn absolution and led the procession from the church to the steps outside and down to the street, where he waited until the remains were placed in the hearse.
>
> Then he came to Mam, took her two hands in his and said, 'You are privileged. You should be the proud mother!', and she said, 'I am!' He said, 'Surely you're not going to journey to Loughglynn?' and Mam said, 'Yes, I wouldn't let her go without me'.
>
> The cortège moved slowly and solemnly to the end of McCurtain Street and then out through Blackpool, past the two houses in Thomas Davis Street and Dublin Street where most of her childhood had been spent. It was this touch that moved me most deeply and I said, 'Moll has arranged all this herself'.

All along the 180-mile journey to Loughglynn people waited in villages and at crossroads, taking off their hats and blessing themselves as the funeral passed by. In the town of Tuam, the Mayor and Council formed a guard of honour and marched with the hearse as far as the town boundary. Night was beginning to fall as the funeral procession reached the convent at Loughglynn and it was met by the nuns of the community wearing white robes and carrying lighted candles in their hands.

The following day was 1 October, Molly's month's mind. After Mass in the convent chapel, the coffin was brought to the small community cemetery, a quarter of a mile from the house. The sun was shining as the mourners walked down the woodland path to the shore of the lake. In that beautiful setting, under the large stone cross in the centre of the graveyard, Molly's remains were finally laid to rest.

The depth of the emotion which her death touched off in the Irish people reflected the tragic circumstances in which it took place. But the tribute they paid her was not merely a personal one. Molly had become a symbol. She represented Irish missionaries everywhere, those who had been expelled from China and other countries, those who had been accused and misrepresented, those who had been imprisoned or tortured or put to death, those who had merely worked away quietly and undramatically through a long lifetime, renewing each day their initial commitment: those who had done their duty.

* * *

The fate of the sisters who remained on in Peking was for many years wrapped in obscurity, as was everything else that happened in China during those years of the Cultural Revolution. Official reports stated that they had been sentenced to twenty years' imprisonment for their activities against the People but no information was available about the place or circumstances of their imprisonment.

It was not until Mao's death in 1976 that normality began to return and the slow and cautious process of dismantling the Cultural Revolution got under way. Many victims of the Red Guards were released from prison and labour camps, rehabilitated and restored to their positions. As it was not possible to attack Mao directly, blame for the excesses was put on his advisers, the so-called Gang of Four, led by Mao's widow. The country began to welcome foreign trade and tourism and even to allow elements of capitalism among its own people.

The official policy continued to be firmly opposed to religion but active persecution was scaled down. During the Cultural Revolution even the Patriotic Catholic churches had been attacked and desecrated. Now they were allowed to open again and conduct services. Those who remained faithful to Rome were still discriminated against. All attempts to bring about a reconciliation between the Patriotic Church and the rest of the Catholic Church were discouraged and blocked by the government.

Early in 1986 a foreign correspondent in Peking, Mark

O'Neill, met an eighty-three-year-old nun living in a hostel in the city. She was a slightly built woman, dressed in patched clothes with a brown headscarf, and she identified herself as Sister Fintana, the nun who had been turned back at the last moment when the other foreign nuns left the Sacred Heart Convent. The story she told him was a sad one.

After the wrecking of the convent, she was taken with about fifty other nuns to a former church, where they were forced to spend their time making toy guns and studying the works of Chairman Mao. They worked sixteen hours a day, with one piece of coarse bread as their daily food allowance. At night they slept on the church benches or on wooden planks. Later, she was given sweet potatoes and buns to eat and a separate cubicle to sleep in, because she was half English.

She asked to be allowed to study Chinese but was refused. Instead, she had to recite the thoughts of Mao in English to her captors, who did not understand a word she was saying. Her only means of communication was to speak French to those Chinese nuns who had some knowledge of it.

Some of her memories of those days were heart-rending. 'I saw a priest and a nun die in front of me', she said, 'after being tortured by Red Guards who wanted them to renounce their faith. They refused. They died as martyrs.'

After Mao's death in 1976 the long ordeal came to an end. Those nuns who were still alive were moved to a former Buddhist temple where they were given more freedom and were even able to set up a little chapel. She began to take pupils for English lessons. In the autumn of 1985 she moved again, this time to a courtyard compound with a chapel. She was still living there at the time of the interview, along with twenty-three other nuns, all over seventy.

'When I see the fervour of Chinese Catholics, I weep for them', she said. 'Perhaps it is because of all they have been through. But China has been good to me except for the Cultural Revolution. I am so happy that religion is free again. I have many pupils of English and I try my best for them for God.'

The publication of this interview was embarrassing to the Chinese authorities. While they were prepared to admit that excesses had been committed under Mao, they did not like the outside world to be reminded of them in too much detail. Other foreigners who tried to get more information about her and other nuns found mysterious obstacles placed in their way. However, a colour photograph that has come into the author's possession from a source in Peking lends support to the story.

The photograph shows a group of elderly Chinese women standing in what appears to be a small courtyard. They are dressed in blue jackets and trousers. In front of them are sitting six men, one dressed as a bishop, another as a priest. In the background are a few young women. Above their heads is a banner in Chinese characters which translates: 'Warm welcome to twenty-two old nuns celebrating fifty years in the convent.'

The official who provided the photograph said that the group included three nuns from the Sacred Heart Convent, the only members of the community still alive. They were living in a home for the elderly but it was not possible for foreigners to talk to them as they were not allowed to receive visitors. The official did not give the names of the three nuns. But conspicuous among the Chinese faces in the photograph is a small grey-haired woman with European features, dressed in a brown coat and brown headscarf. She exactly matches Mark O'Neill's description of Sister Fintana.

The convent building was still standing in 1986, though in a half-ruined condition. After the expulsion of the nuns, it was used for a period by the Peking Municipal Bureau of Textiles before they moved to new premises. Thereafter it remained unoccupied except for a caretaker. Some damage was caused to the upper storeys by an earthquake in 1976 and the decision was made to demolish the building. Demolition work was still going on in 1986 but in a manner so half-hearted that it could continue until the end of the century.

What was left of the building appeared structurally sound and it was hard to avoid thinking that the decision to demolish it was based on political rather than architectural reasons. The Sacred Heart Convent symbolises an era in Chinese history which the authorities would like people to forget.

EPILOGUE

Writing a life is a work of selection. Stacked around me at the moment are folders of Molly's letters, arranged by months and years, more than 350 of them altogether. To print them all would need half a dozen books the size of this one. All the biographer can do is select extracts which seem to represent accurately the subject as he sees her.

It would be easy to make a different selection. It would be easy to pick pieces which highlighted her good qualities and concealed her defects. It would be easy to picture her as a latter-day saint and martyr. No major falsification would be needed: nothing more than the occasional discreet omission or correction. Her faults of temper and temperament could be passed over in silence. Her times of depression could be interpreted in terms of the dark night of St John of the Cross. Her slapdash style of writing, never intended for publication, could be polished up and spiritualised as was done with the best of intentions in the case of St Thérèse of Lisieux. Her references to her increasing weight would have to be ignored; with the possible exception of St Thomas Aquinas, there has never been a fat saint.

The picture thus built up would be edifying and plausible, but it would not be true. None of those who knew Molly ever saw her as anyone exceptional. None of them was ever tempted to canonise her, least of all herself. She was a shrewd judge of her own character and she knew that, whatever else she was, she was certainly not a saint. In a revealing letter written to her mother in 1955, she spoke about her irritability. 'Small things annoy me. And then I get annoyed because these small things have power to annoy me.' She then went on to say that some distant relations had written to her out of the blue, apparently under the impression that their cousin toiling away among the perils of Red China must be some kind of a saint:

> I was flabbergasted. I thought all these had forgotten my existence. But says I to myself says I, 'Maybe I have a halo now', for various reasons. To be sure, faraway cows wear long horns. I imagine they are rather proud of their cousin. It is no fault of the cousin's. She is simply doing her duty and in spots it is rather pleasant.

That phrase 'She is simply doing her duty' sums up her whole philosophy of life. If she were asked what epitaph she would like to have written on her tombstone, I think she would be very well pleased with 'She did her duty'. She made one great decision in her life, the decision to offer herself to God as a Franciscan Missionary of Mary. Everything else followed from that. Everything else was her renewal of that decision and of that offering, her daily living out of the consequences. She had made her commitment and to carry it out was no more than her duty.

Her fifty-nine years on earth can be summed up very simply: twenty-eight years in Cork and twenty-eight years in Peking, separated by three years of novitiate. Her childhood and youth in Cork formed her character and her outlook. She inherited something of her father's gentleness and something of her mother's steel. From both of them and from the Ireland in which she grew up, she inherited her rock-steady religious belief and moral values.

Her family and her country gave Molly security and happiness of a kind that is not often found today. They gave her something more: they gave her the strength to turn her back on that security and happiness and to take the long road that led to the bridge at Lo Wu. Her decision to enter the convent at Loughglynn was the crucial event of her life. Everything that went before led up to it, everything that came after flowed from it.

From then on, she was subject to obedience. She thought she would never have to make another such decision. The will of her superiors would decide everything for her. As events turned out, there were to be two more moments of decision. One was in Rome in 1938, when the killing of the nuns in China became known and Molly was told she could turn back if she wished. The other was in Peking in 1948 when she was given the option of leaving before the communists took over. There is no evidence that she agonised over either decision. She was not the type to put her hand to the plough and then turn back.

In this too she was not exceptional. There were many others of her generation whose faith and endurance were the equal of hers. It was an accident of history that led to her brief moment of fame, when she was trundled across the Hong Kong border before the eyes and cameras of the world. We can call her a typical representative of what was best in the missionaries of her time. We cannot call her a saint, unless we are to call all of them saints.